CW01334721

TIVETSHALL TO BECCLES

Richard Adderson and
Graham Kenworthy

Series editor Vic Mitchell

MP Middleton Press

Cover picture. A typical three-coach train waits at Bungay's up platform behind class F4 2-4-2T no.67158 on 21st July 1952. Two vehicles of GER origin flank an LNER non-corridor composite coach. Through the gate we see a solitary passenger trudging up the hill from the station on her way home. (Mid-Rail Photographs)

Published September 2004

ISBN 1 904474 41 1

© Middleton Press, 2004

Design David Pede

Published by
        Middleton Press
        Easebourne Lane
        Midhurst, West Sussex
        GU29 9AZ
Tel: 01730 813169
Fax: 01730 812601
Email: info@middletonpress.co.uk
www.middletonpress.co.uk

Printed & bound by Biddles Ltd, Kings Lynn

INDEX

Beccles	115	Homersfield	46
Bungay	65	Pulham Market	8
Ditchingham	91	Pulham Mary	16
Earsham	59	Redenhall	41
Ellingham	100	Starston	24
Geldeston	107	Tivetshall	1
Harleston	26	Wortwell	44

ACKNOWLEDGEMENTS

In addition to the individuals acknowledged in the photographic credits, we are most grateful to the following people for their assistance in the compilation of this book; S.Allen, F.Tanner, M.Rayner, C.Reeve, A.Rush, and M.Storey-Smith. The Great Eastern Railway Society has produced a series of CDs of material to be found in the National Archive at Kew; these have proved extremely useful in researching detailed background information.

Readers of this book may be interested in the following society:
Great Eastern Railway Society
J.R.Tant
Membership Secretary
9 Clare Road
Leytonstone
London E11 1JU

Railways of the area in 1952 at a scale of approx. 1 inch to 5 miles. Other plans in this volume are to a scale of 25 ins to 1 mile, unless otherwise stated.

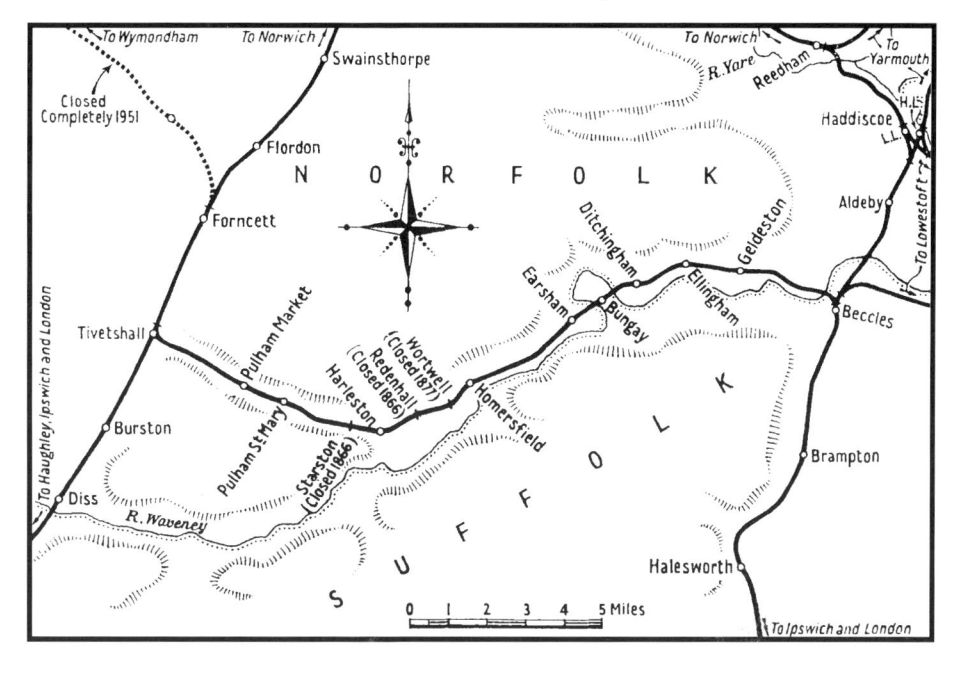

GEOGRAPHICAL SETTING

While "Waveney Valley Branch" has always been a convenient name to apply to the line, the reference is slightly misleading, in that little more than 50% of the branch was located in the valley. At the western end of the line, this river, which marks the boundary between Norfolk and Suffolk, lies some six miles to the south, passing through Diss.

From the junction at Tivetshall, which is located at a summit on the main line between Diss and Norwich, the branch veered away almost due eastwards to follow the course of a stream, locally known as the "Beck", to Homersfield, the point of confluence with the Waveney. From there on, the route of the railway is rarely more than a few hundred yards from the Waveney as it follows what is, at times, a rather meandering course along the broad valley. Apart from brief incursions into Suffolk at Bungay and again near the junction at Beccles, the line was entirely in Norfolk.

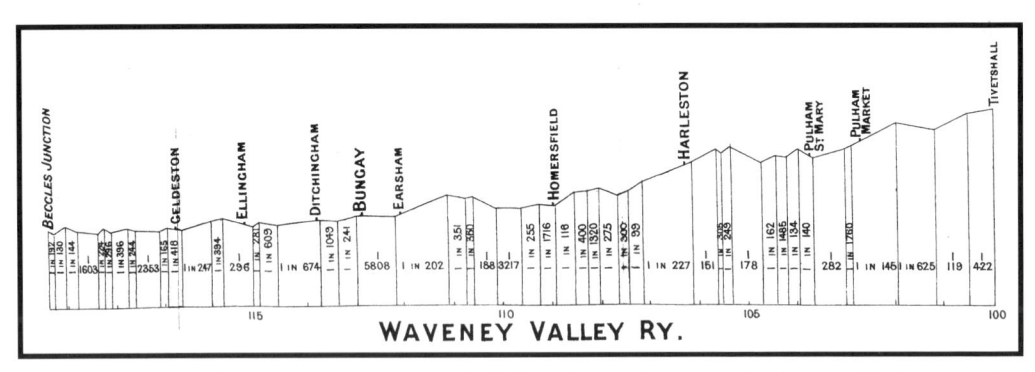

The gradient diagram dates from the early GER period and is, unusually, drawn with the increasing mileage from right to left. The mileage used is that from Bishopsgate (the early London terminus) via Ipswich and Tivetshall. The opening of Liverpool Street increased these mileages by about ½ mile.

HISTORICAL BACKGROUND

The wide valley of the River Waveney, stretching inland for over thirty miles from the ports of Lowestoft and Yarmouth, would have provided an extremely easy and direct first stage in linking them with London by rail. However proposals in the mid-1840s to take advantage of this potentially benevolent geographical feature were met with a series of objections and refusals too complex to detail here. Suffice to say that a series of more successful schemes completed between 1845 and 1849, rendered the Waveney Valley option unviable as a main line.

When an acceptable scheme serving the area was finally authorised in July 1851, it took the form of a purely local branch linking Bungay with the Eastern Union Railway's main line at Tivetshall. A further Act was obtained in August 1853 for an extension eastwards from Bungay to the embryonic Halesworth, Beccles and Haddiscoe Railway at Beccles. The line opened in stages, from Tivetshall to Harleston on 1 December 1855, from Harleston to Bungay on 2 November 1860, and the final section from Bungay to Beccles on 2 March 1863.

During this later construction period the Waveney Valley Railway Company was absorbed into the Great Eastern Railway on its formation in August 1862. The Great Eastern Railway became part of the London & North Eastern Railway on 1st January 1923.

The later years of World War II saw a considerable upsurge in traffic, both pasenger and freight, due to the establishment of a number of strategic military installations close to the line. However this counted for nought when the branch became part of the Eastern Region of British Railways upon nationalisation on 1st January 1948. The passenger service was one of the victims of the post-nationalisation purge of the early 1950s, withdrawal taking place on 5th January 1953.

At first the whole route remained open for freight, but, because it had connections to the national network at both ends, the service pattern varied from time to time. This situation changed towards the end of 1960, when the central section, between Harleston and Bungay closed, following withdrawal of facilities from Homersfield earlier in the year. The next section to be abandoned was that from Ditchingham to Bungay in August 1964, followed by Beccles to Ditchingham in August 1965. The final closure was from Tivetshall to Harleston in April 1966. Dates of withdrawal of freight services from individual stations can be found in the photographic captions.

PASSENGER SERVICES

Broadly speaking, the demands of the local population, whether in Summer or Winter, triggered very little change in the number of trains provided during the entire lifetime of the passenger service. Surprisingly enough, the number of trains reached its zenith during the first two years of World War I. With the exception of the references to the early level of services, only trains running each weekday are quoted in the following brief details. At least two Sunday excursions were run during the final summer of passenger operation, but, apart from occasional similar workings over the years, few trains were provided to disturb the peace of a Waveney Valley sabbath;

An Eastern Counties Railway timetable for September 1856, when the line was only open from Tivetshall to Harleston, showed four return trains on weekdays in each direction with the first trip starting from Harleston at 7.35 am and the last returning from Tivetshall at 8.25 pm.

This level of service was maintained by the Great Eastern Railway in 1865, early in the life of the completed route. The timetable for June that year also showed four weekday trains in each direction (plus an additional up train early on Mondays together with other services on Norwich Market Days). The only intermediate stations at which trains were booked to stop were Harleston, Homersfield and Bungay; the other nine stations were classed as request stops only, but, even so, not all trains were given authority to stop at all such stations.

By contrast, by October 1915, the number of trains had reached a peak of eight in each direction over the full length of the branch: seven of these were extended to and from Norwich Thorpe at the Tivetshall end. There was another service which ran only from Beccles to Harleston and back.

The ongoing demands of World War I reduced this level to six in each direction (with four of them through to Norwich) from January 1917. The Winter timetable of 1926/7 showed an identical level of service.

Six trains per day was still the order of the day in the Summer of 1950 but with only three extended to/from Norwich Thorpe.

By 1953, the year of passenger closure, the number of services had remained unaltered for 36 years.

1893

TIVETSHALL

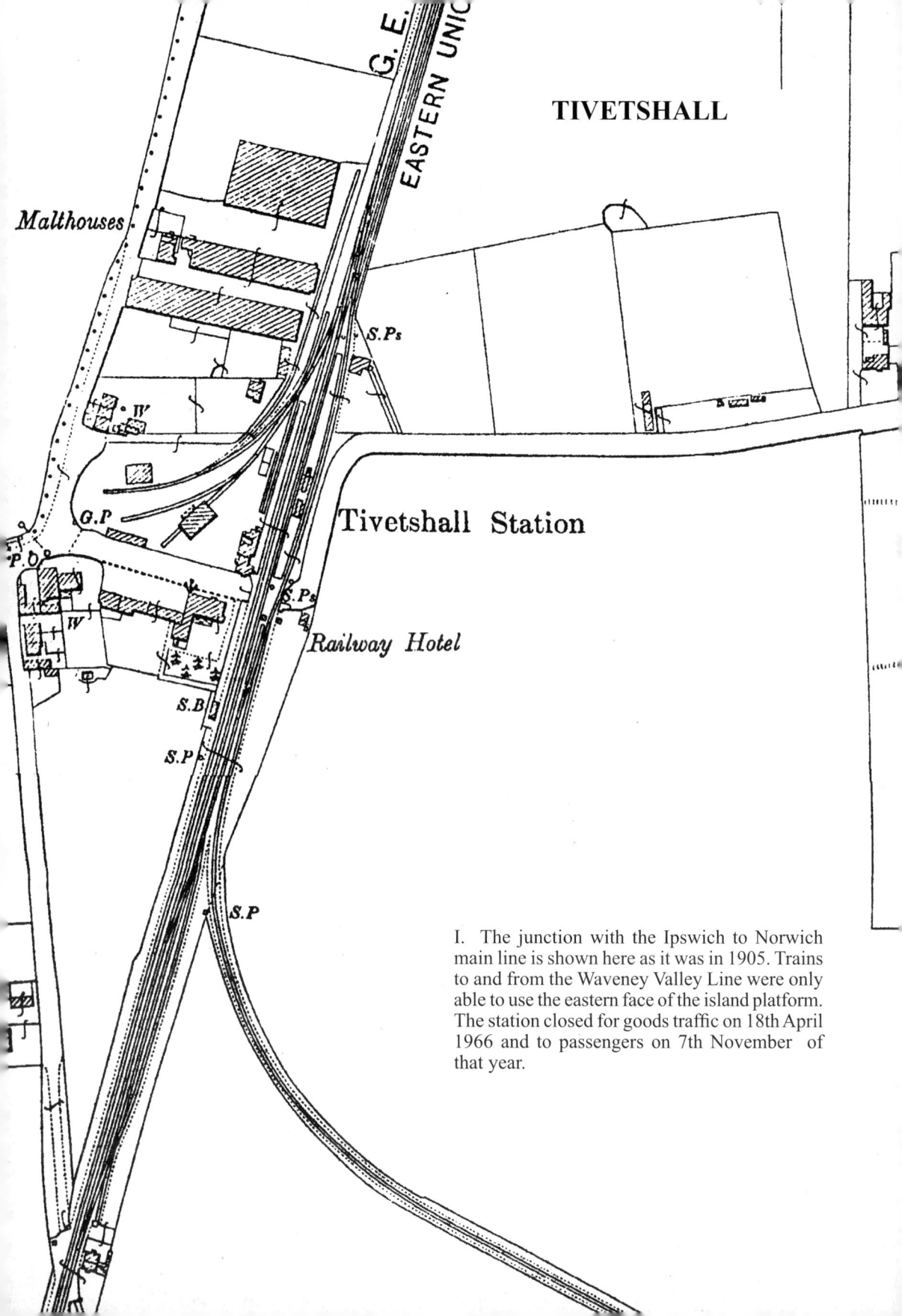

Malthouses

Tivetshall Station

Railway Hotel

1. The junction with the Ipswich to Norwich main line is shown here as it was in 1905. Trains to and from the Waveney Valley Line were only able to use the eastern face of the island platform. The station closed for goods traffic on 18th April 1966 and to passengers on 7th November of that year.

1. The comprehensive running-in board on the down platform greeted passengers until early 1953, and welcomes us to a journey along one of East Anglia's most rural branch lines. Over half of the communities served by the line are honoured with a mention.
(A.G.Forsyth/Initial Photographics)

2. Class B1 4-6-0 no. 61054 passes the signal box as it slows for the station stop with the 8.55 am train from Ipswich to Norwich on 1st September 1951. This train was booked to call at all the intermediate stations, and its 46¼ mile journey occupied 105 minutes. The Waveney Valley branch curves away to the extreme left of the picture. (H.C.Casserley)

3. On a sunny Winter day in the early 1950s, a stopping train stands at the down platform, while an ex-GER 2-4-2T waits with the branch line connection. Two railwaymen are having a chat, but there is no sign of any passengers. (Stations UK)

4. We are now looking northwards from the signal box, again around 1951. The water tower, which supplied the three water columns on the platforms, is on the right. Between the two signals, we can see a rake of coaches, stabled in the sidings that had been installed during World War II to handle traffic to the bomber bases in the area. (B.D.J.Walsh)

5. The main lines and branch had separate sets of crossing gates at the south end of the platform. We are standing on the island platform on a dull day in the early 1960s as the goods train for Harleston negotiates the sharp curve away from the main line. (NRS Archive)

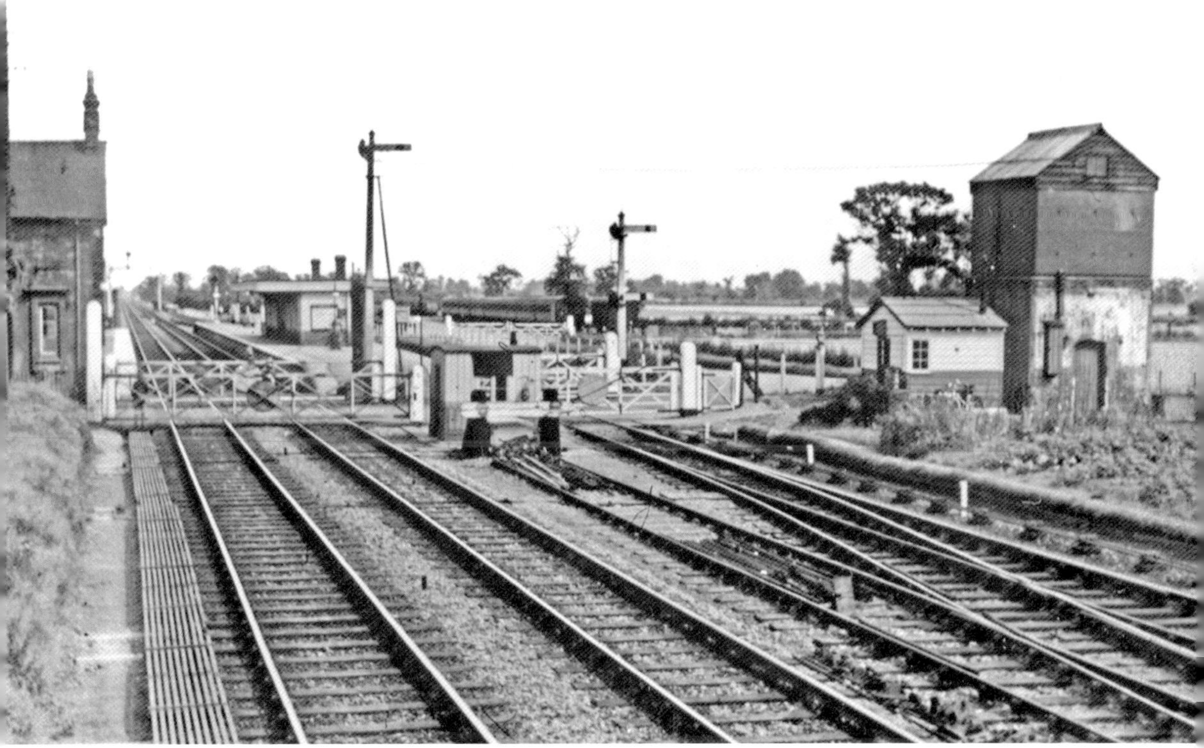

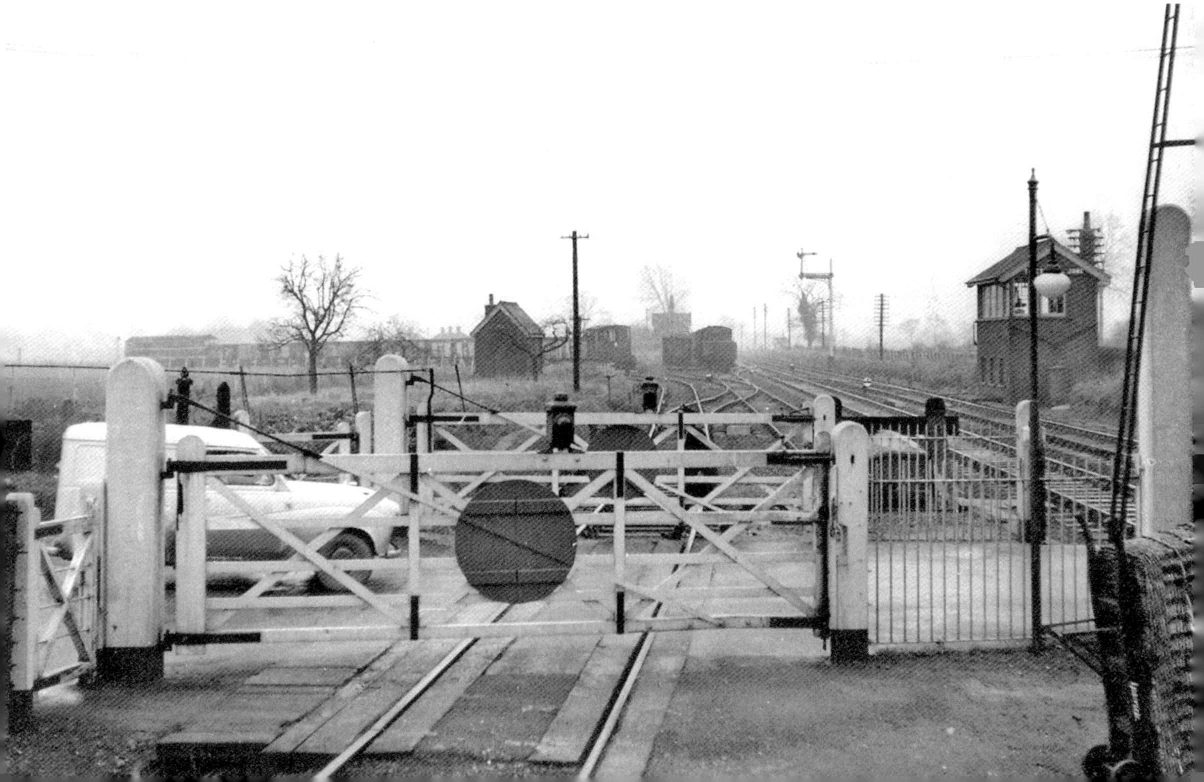

EAST OF TIVETSHALL

6. During the last years of operation, the daily goods train for Harleston waits while a member of the train crew closes the level crossing gates to traffic on the A140. There were no less than four level crossings in the first two miles out of Tivetshall but this one, on the main road from Norwich to Ipswich, was by far the best known. (Pictorail/Ryan)

7. Now we are looking eastwards towards the A140 on 3rd July 1966, some 10 weeks after the final closure. Following the withdrawal of passenger services, the line had been operated as a light railway, and most of the level crossings over country lanes had lost their gates. This could not be permitted at the busy main road, and indeed a new set of gates had been required as the result of road widening. (Railway Record of the British Isles/G.L.Pring)

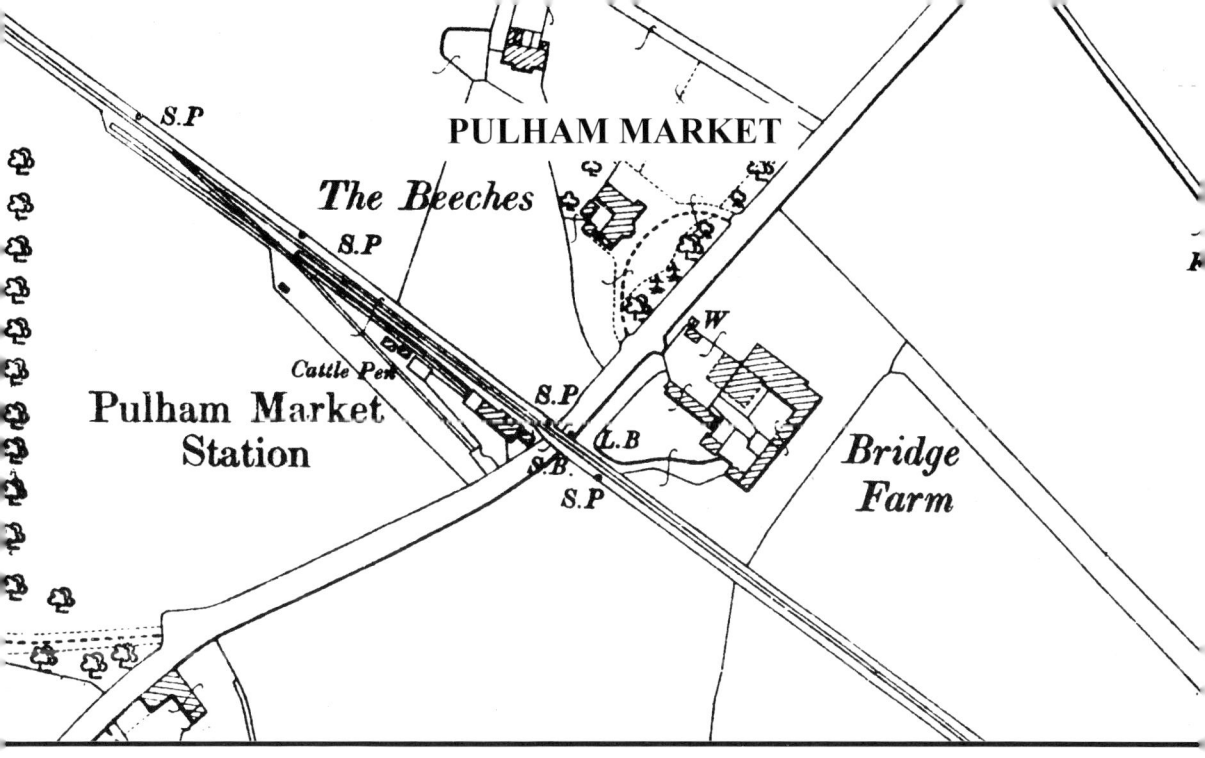

II. This station appeared in the first timetables as Pulham St.Magdalene, but, within a few months, had acquired the title it bore for the rest of its life. Apart from the earlier lengthenings of the platform, this 1905 plan shows broadly the situation that existed at this station for around one hundred years.

8. During its heyday, the railway was a major employer, even in rural districts. On this occasion, the workforce has congregated for the photographer in front of the station building. It is likely that the three men in waistcoats are the local track gang, and the other four are the staff employed at the station. The poster detailing important alterations to the train service with effect from May 1910 enables us to date the picture. (P.Standley collection)

9. Forty years later, there are just two railwaymen in the picture, standing by the meticulously maintained fence. We are looking from the south-east, across the road. (HMRS)

G. E. R.

Pulham Market

10. Just to the east of the station, a long siding headed southwards to Pulham airfield, where a network of 2ft. gauge lines connected with the airfield installations. This was a major airship base, and was home to the R33 and R34 between the wars. The line was constructed for the Admiralty during 1915, and survived until the airfield closed in 1958. Class N7 0-6-2T no. 67679 stands on the siding with a goods train around 1951. The oval plate on the sleeper marks the boundary between BR and what had become Air Ministry property. (Dr I.C.Allen/The Transport Treasury)

11. As no trains are expected, we can look eastwards along the track towards the level crossing, just before the passenger closure. A few wagons loaded with sugar beet are standing in the siding beyond the 300 feet long platform, awaiting the arrival of the goods train. (Stations UK)

12. The platform was originally no more than 99 feet long, and was extended by 30 feet in 1885, before a final lengthening in 1892. Right up to closure, the narrowing of the platform revealed the starting point of the 1892 work, as this picture from the early 1960s proves. (Stations UK)

13. The train seen in picture 6 has negotiated the A140, and it is again the responsibility of the train crew to operate the level crossing gates. By this time the signal box had long been demolished. (Pictorail/Ryan)

14. Goods facilities were withdrawn from 13th July 1964, and the last train passed the station on its way back from Harleston in April 1966. Tracklifting began in early 1968, and this was the scene on 10th September 1971. The building still has a future, as there is new brickwork on the eastern end, and the area underneath the awning has been integrated into the main structure. (H.C.Casserley)

15. Another 30 years have passed, and the station building is still there. A satellite dish is a sign of the times, whilst the signal serves as a reminder of the past. (G.L.Kenworthy)

PULHAM ST. MARY

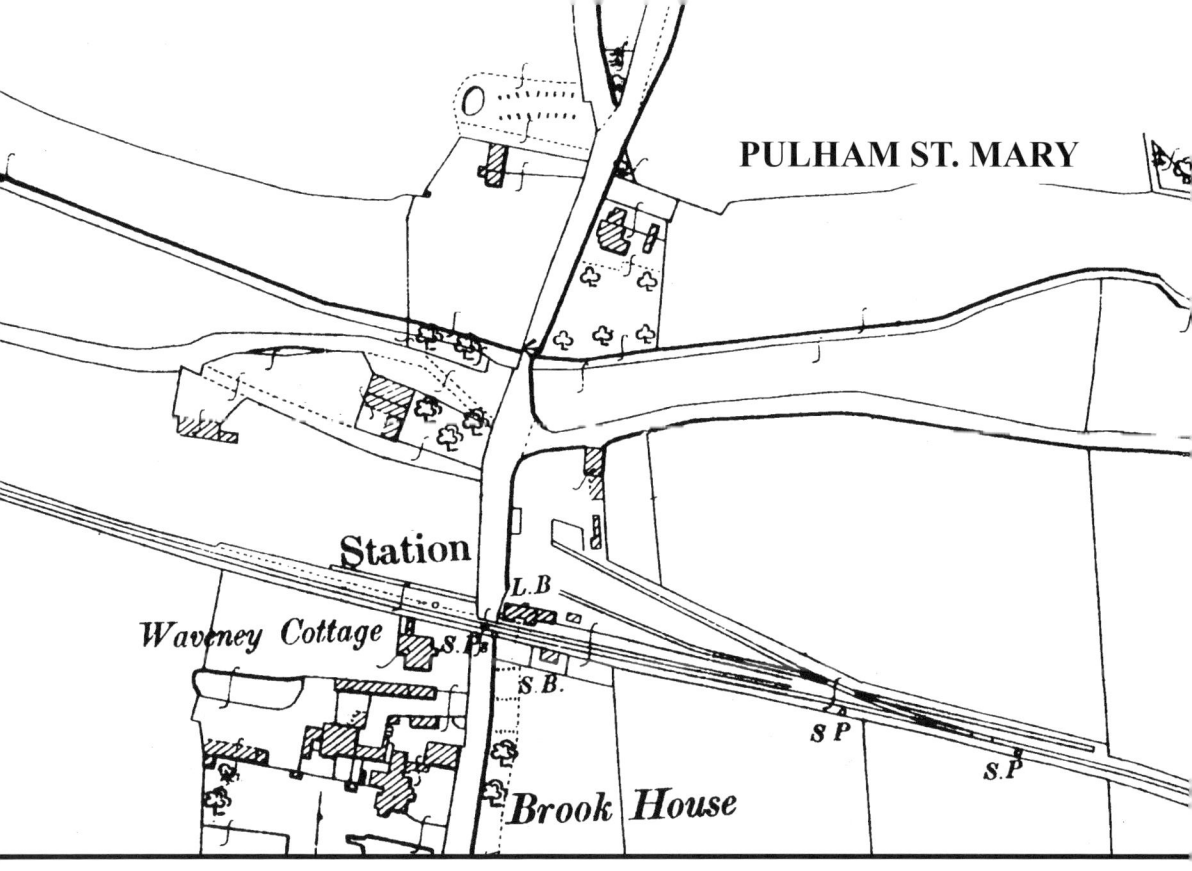

III. As far as the various railway authorities, not to mention the local staff, were concerned, there always seemed to be a question mark hanging over Mary's canonisation! The "St." was present in as many instances as it was omitted. The "Beck", the watercourse followed by the line at its western end, is located a few yards to the north of, and parallel to, the railway. The village lies further to the north, on higher ground. The plan dates from 1905.

16. A resting cyclist provides the only sign of life as we look south along Station Road on a sunny morning around 1910. Framed between the trees, the station building forms an integral part of the scene. (P.Standley collection)

17. We make our way to the south side of the line, to find two ladies in long dresses and splendid hats standing on the platform. Housekeeping here had been the subject of criticism in earlier years. The GER minutes reveal that the coal used for heating stations in the year to June 1866 averaged two tons per fire. However, this station managed to consume over seven tons per fire, prompting the comment that "Stationmasters are not supplied with coal for private use."
(P.Standley collection)

18. The main station building was similar to that at the other Pulham, but the signal box stood on the south side of the line, opposite the platform.   Four railway employees appear in the picture, together with a canine friend. (P.Standley collection)

19. This is the signalbox interior, around 1951. A frame of 15 levers, of which four were spare, is large enough to meet the signalling requirements of the location. (B.D.J.Walsh)

20. A host of details bring the station to life. The oil lamps, weighing machine, timetable posters, platform barrows, seats and even the cast iron "Gentlemen" sign, combine to animate the scene, even though there are no people in sight. Most of these items will disappear within a year or two, when the passenger service stops. (Stations UK)

21. The place is still very tidy a decade or so later, on 31st July 1961, and the track seems to be well maintained. However, all the details shown in the previous picture have gone, and the brick base of the demolished signalbox adds to the lifelessness of the scene, even though goods traffic was handled until 13th July 1964. (J.Watling)

22.   The railway company was always ready to make use of redundant carriage bodies when their passenger carrying days were over, either by selling them to private individuals or by using them as sheds, storehouses and, occasionally, station buildings. Two such bodies are rotting gently in the station yard on 3rd July 1966. The nearer body dates from the late 1890s, whilst the further is a decade or more older. (Railway Record of the British Isles/G.L.Pring)

23.   The station was left to decay after the line was abandoned in April 1966. Bushes are spreading across the crumbling platform, the track is overgrown, and two broken windows tell their own story of neglect on 29th October 1967. The station building was later demolished. (R.J.Adderson)

STARSTON

IV. The remains of one of the stations which closed early in the life of the line is shown as it existed in 1905; along with Redenhall it closed on 1st August 1866. For a parish with only 485 inhabitants at the time of opening, it is rather surprising that the service survived for over ten years.

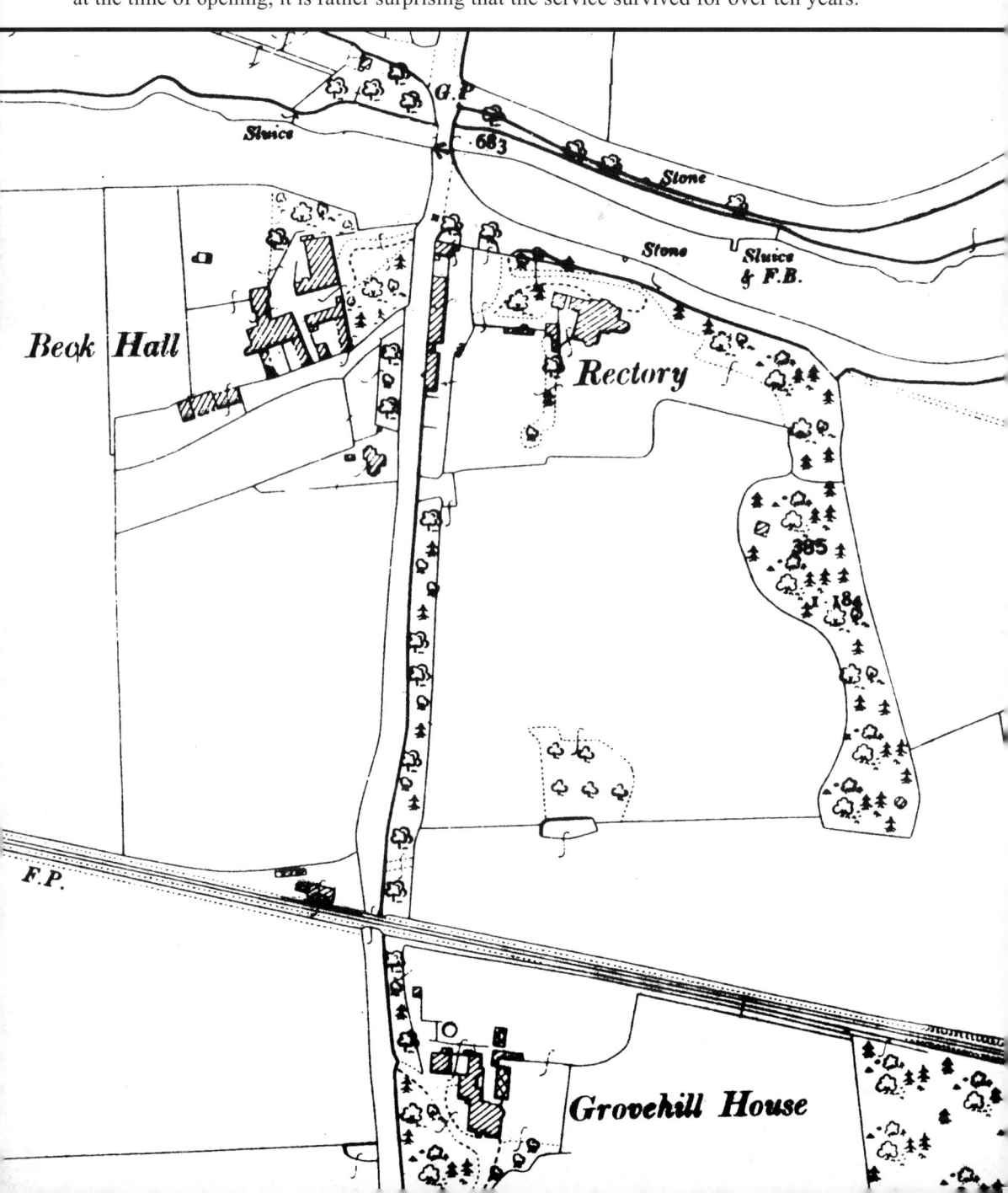

24. An 1856 timetable shows this to be one of three intermediate stations on the "Harlestone branch", which were served when required. (The other two were the Pulham stations.) Despite a brief life of no more than eleven years, the station building remained intact beside the track in 1954. (Stations UK)

25. Half a century later, the traveller can turn off the main road in Starston and make his way up Railway Hill - a subtle variation from the ubiquitous Station Road - to find the unmistakable station building still overlooking the village. This was the approach from the north in November 2001. (G.L.Kenworthy)

HARLESTON

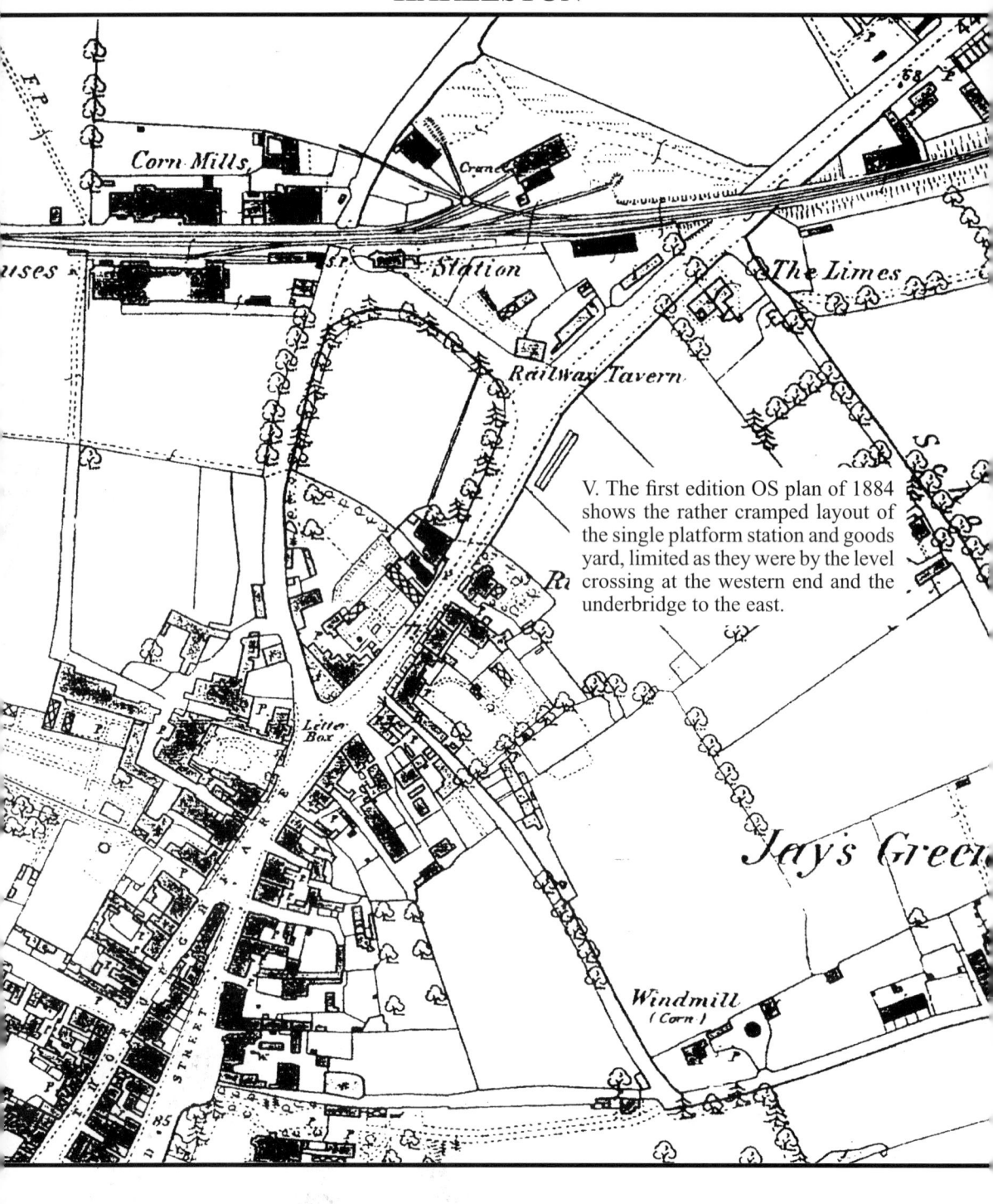

V. The first edition OS plan of 1884 shows the rather cramped layout of the single platform station and goods yard, limited as they were by the level crossing at the western end and the underbridge to the east.

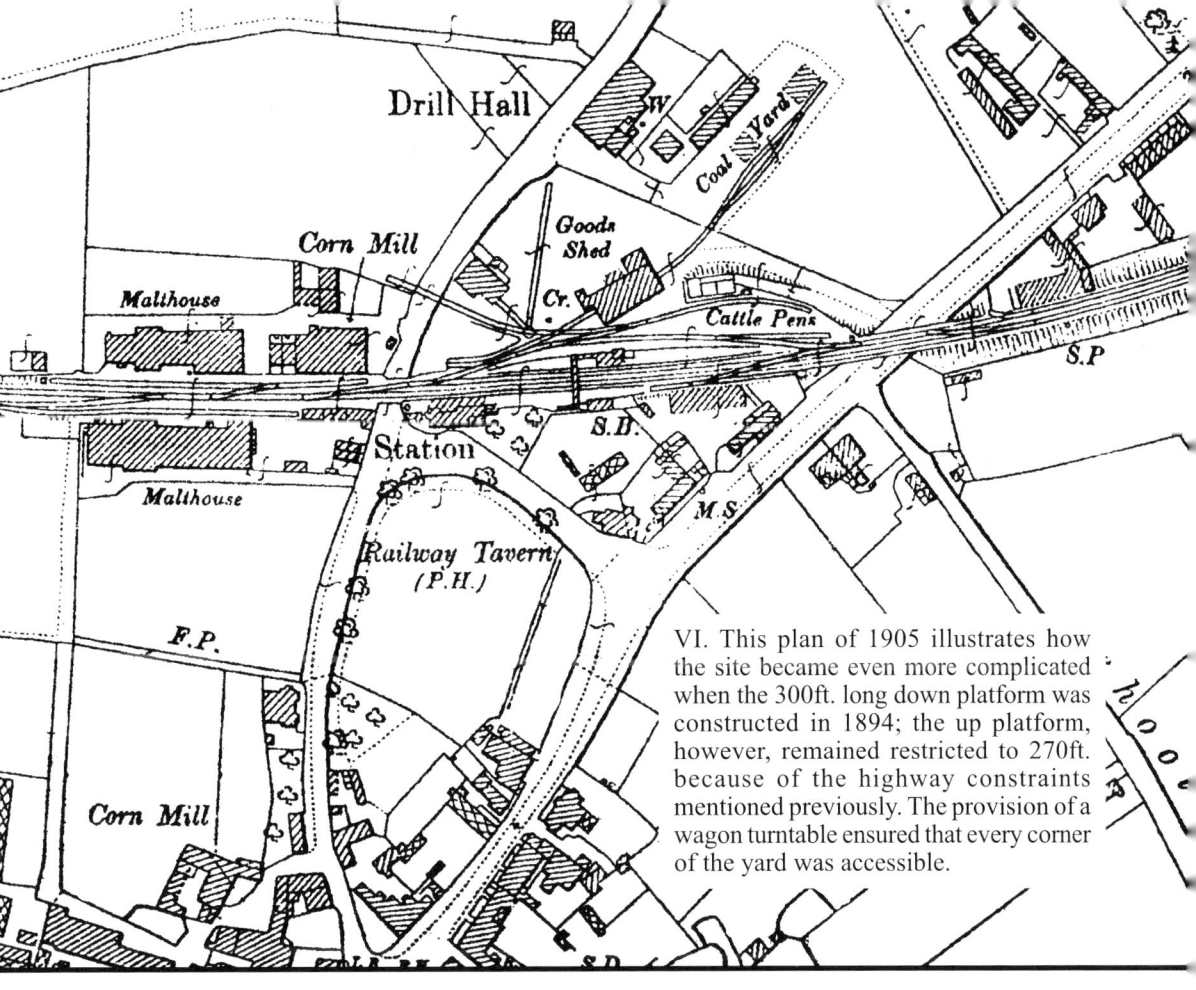

VI. This plan of 1905 illustrates how the site became even more complicated when the 300ft. long down platform was constructed in 1894; the up platform, however, remained restricted to 270ft. because of the highway constraints mentioned previously. The provision of a wagon turntable ensured that every corner of the yard was accessible.

26. A locally produced postcard provides us with an excellent overall view of the passenger station, with a good number of passengers waiting to board the train which is arriving from the Beccles direction. Another engine is standing in the goods yard, whilst the four workers on the down platform can only be posing for the camera! The card is postmarked 21st September 1904. (P.Standley collection)

27. The Norfolk/Suffolk borders suffered badly from flooding in August 1912. A bus service replaced the trains between here and Bungay – and we shall see the reasons for this later. The GER bus, registration F 2441, is the centre of attention in the station forecourt.
(P.Standley collection)

28. We are looking westwards from the down platform around 1923. With its large 42-lever signal box and impressive range of buildings the station looks prosperous, as befits a market town of some 2000 inhabitants. It was the only station on the line to boast a footbridge.
(Stations UK)

29. A class E4 2-4-0 blocks the level crossing with an up passenger train, as a varied quartet of road vehicles waits in front of the station building. This picture dates from the early days of the LNER. (P.Standley collection)

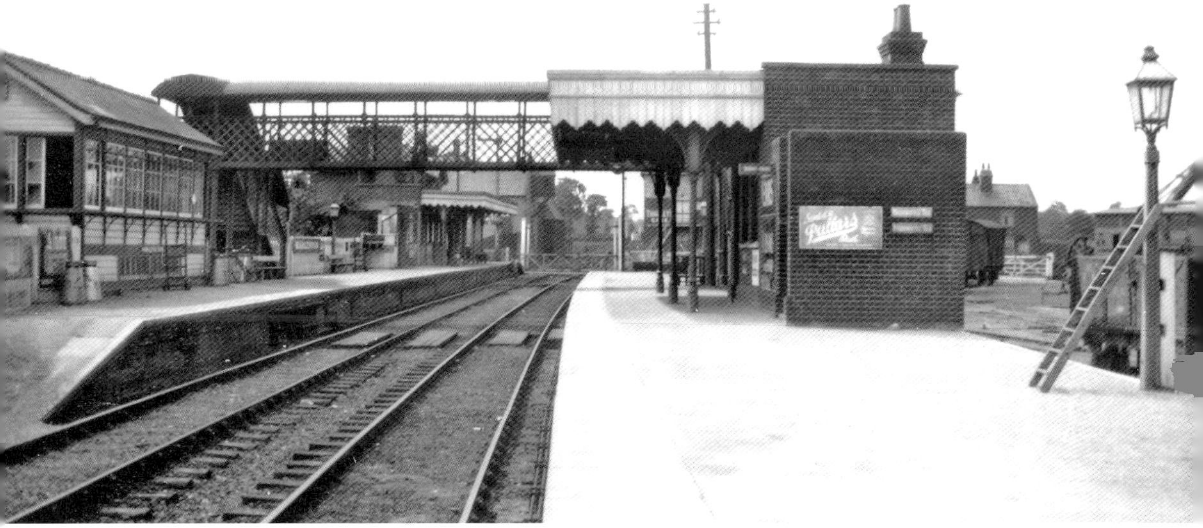

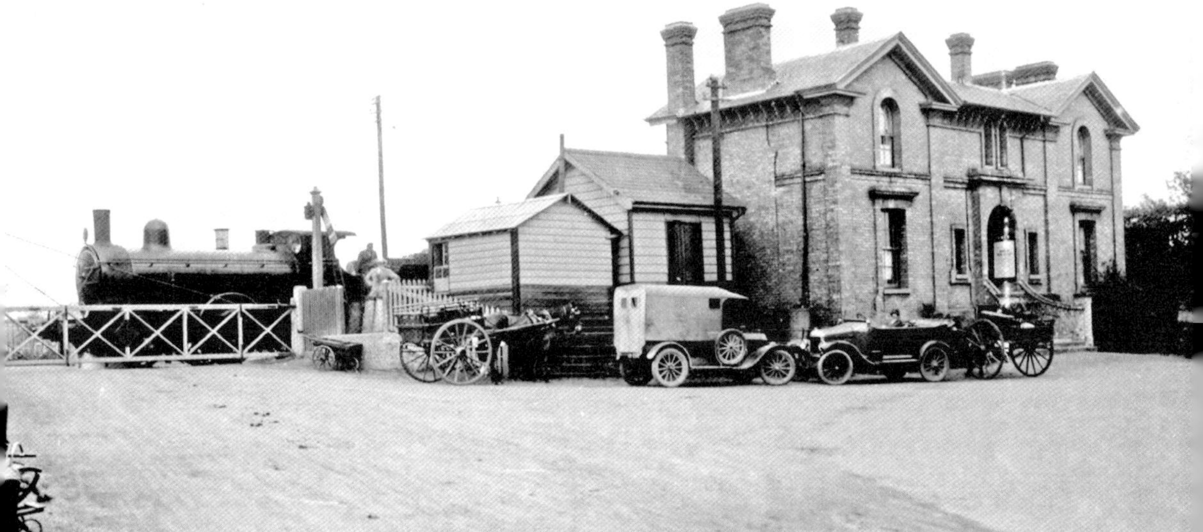

30. We move forward in time to the early 1950s, as a class J15 0-6-0 runs somewhat smokily into the platform with a train for Tivetshall. Plenty of passengers are waiting to pile into the four coaches, and there are at least two prams to be fitted into the guards van. (B.D.J.Walsh)

31. The photographer leans out of the 9 am train from Beccles on 1st September 1951 to record the scene looking eastwards. A corrugated iron roof protects the footbridge from the elements, and the goods shed is on the left, with its huge sliding door open to allow access for rail traffic. (H.C.Casserley)

32. Class J15 0-6-0 no. 65389 has arrived with a goods train, again in the early 1950s. The shunter crosses the line with his pole, ready for the coupling and uncoupling operations, while a small boy prepares to savour the spectacle from the platform end. 65389 bears a 32C (Lowestoft) shedplate, so the train is probably the 9.05 am from Lowestoft, which was scheduled to arrive here at 1.48 pm after shunting at most stations en route. (Bungay Museum/Frank Honeywood collection)

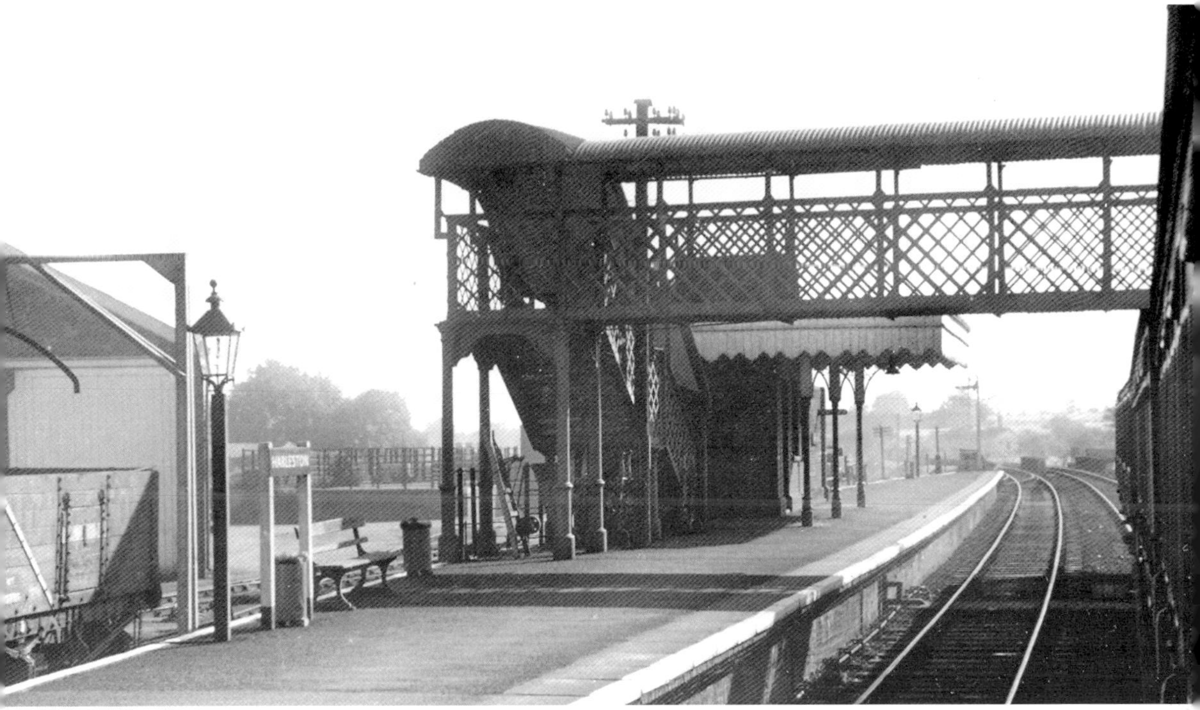
HARLESTON

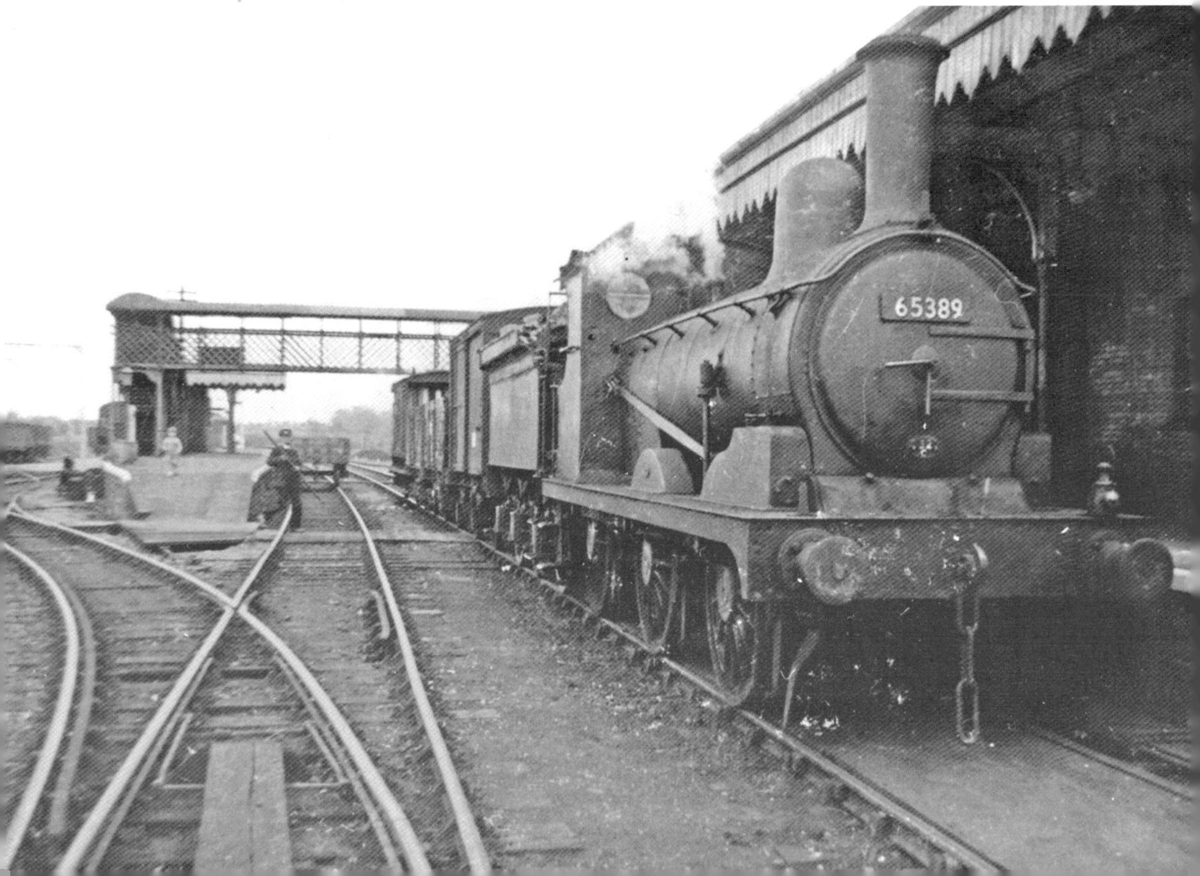
65389

33. Two passenger trains traversed the freight only line during September 1956. A Norfolk Railway Society special worked eastwards on the 8th, followed by the Railway Enthusiasts Club "Suffolk Venturer" which headed in the opposite direction 22 days later. Looking rather odd with an express passenger headcode, class J15 0-6-0 no. 65447 heads the second train. The station has changed little, nearly four years after closure to passenger trains, and the footbridge is still able to take the weight of at least seven people. (Photomatic)

34. We have already seen a variety of vehicles outside the station in pictures nos. 27 and 29. To continue the theme, we see two ageing cars, and a more modern van, as enthusiasts gather round 65447 on 30th September 1956. The demolition of the wooden buildings to the left has revealed the full splendour of the building. (R.M.Casserley)

35. The M&GN Preservation Society Railtour of 8th October 1960 heads east towards the station. By this time, the line through the up platform had been lifted, and the down platform had been demolished. Despite the novelty of a steam hauled passenger train, there is only one photographer waiting on the isolated platform to record the event. (P.G.Rayner)

GOODS & PASSENGER TRAIN
PARCELS OFFICE
FAR-NORTH
FAR-NORTH
BEST PASTES

36. The tracks to the right of the picture outline the site of the down platform, as we look eastwards on 25th March 1961. Goods traffic lingers on: several wagons are dotted around the yard, and a British Railways delivery lorry stands in the shadow of the goods shed, whose rail entrance has been bricked up. (J.Watling)

37. With the closure of the line eastwards in 1960, the station became the terminus of a daily freight train from Tivetshall. At first this ran to and from Norwich, but in later years the 5.10 am goods from Ipswich made a diversion down the branch in the course of its eight-hour trip to Norwich. No. D8202 has arrived with a few wagons during the early 1960s and is shunting at the west end of the station. (P.G.Rayner)

38. The somewhat complex trackwork in the goods yard is again apparent in this view dating from 3rd June 1966. By now the station building is looking very bare from the railway side, having lost the canopy. Although goods traffic was boosted by a regular flow of agricultural machinery from here in the final years, the station closed completely on 18th April 1966. (J.Watling)

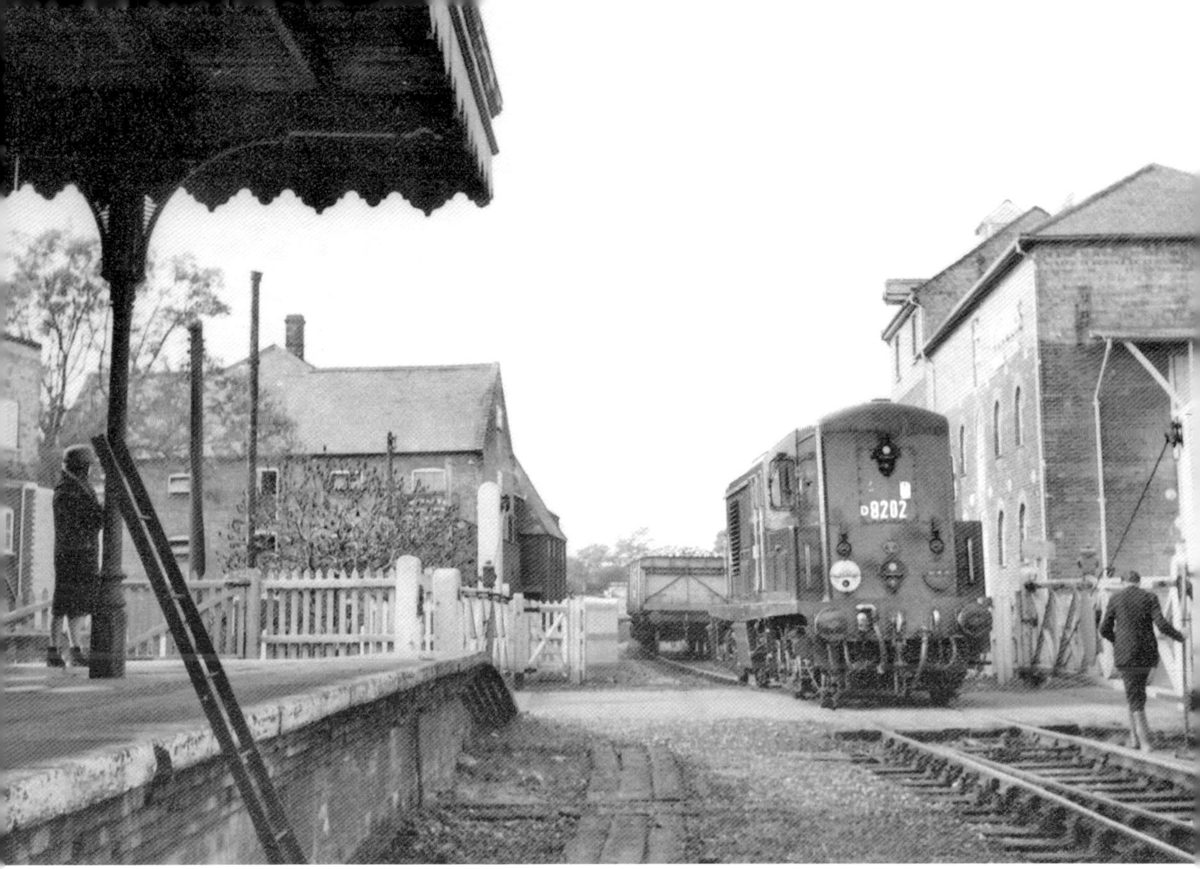
D8202

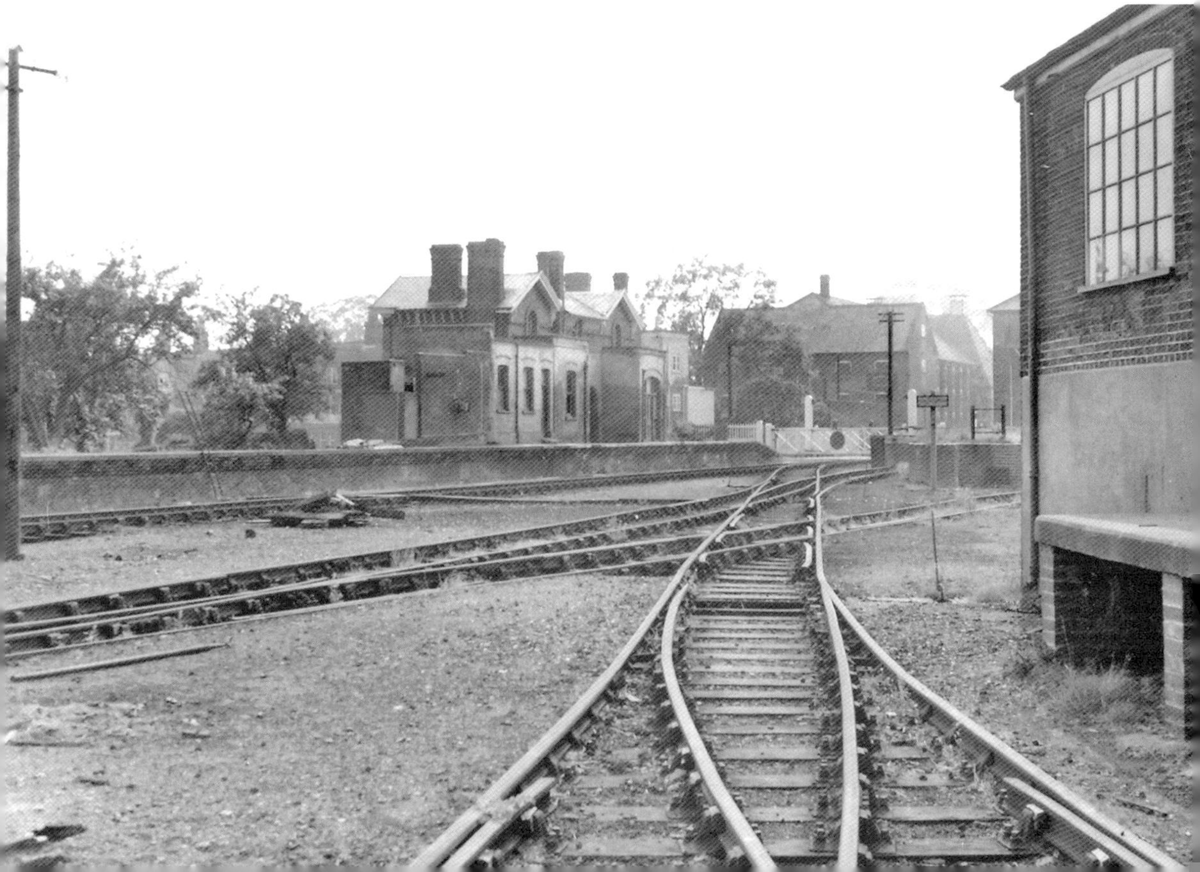

39. Its useful life over, the crane stands forlornly in the goods yard on 3rd June 1966. The name of the makers, Hurwood & Turner, of St Peter's Foundry, Ipswich, is cast into the side. (J.Watling)

40. The station building achieved listed status, and is consequently well maintained, serving as office accommodation. Yet another generation of road vehicle is standing outside the handsome structure in November 2001. (G.L.Kenworthy)

REDENHALL

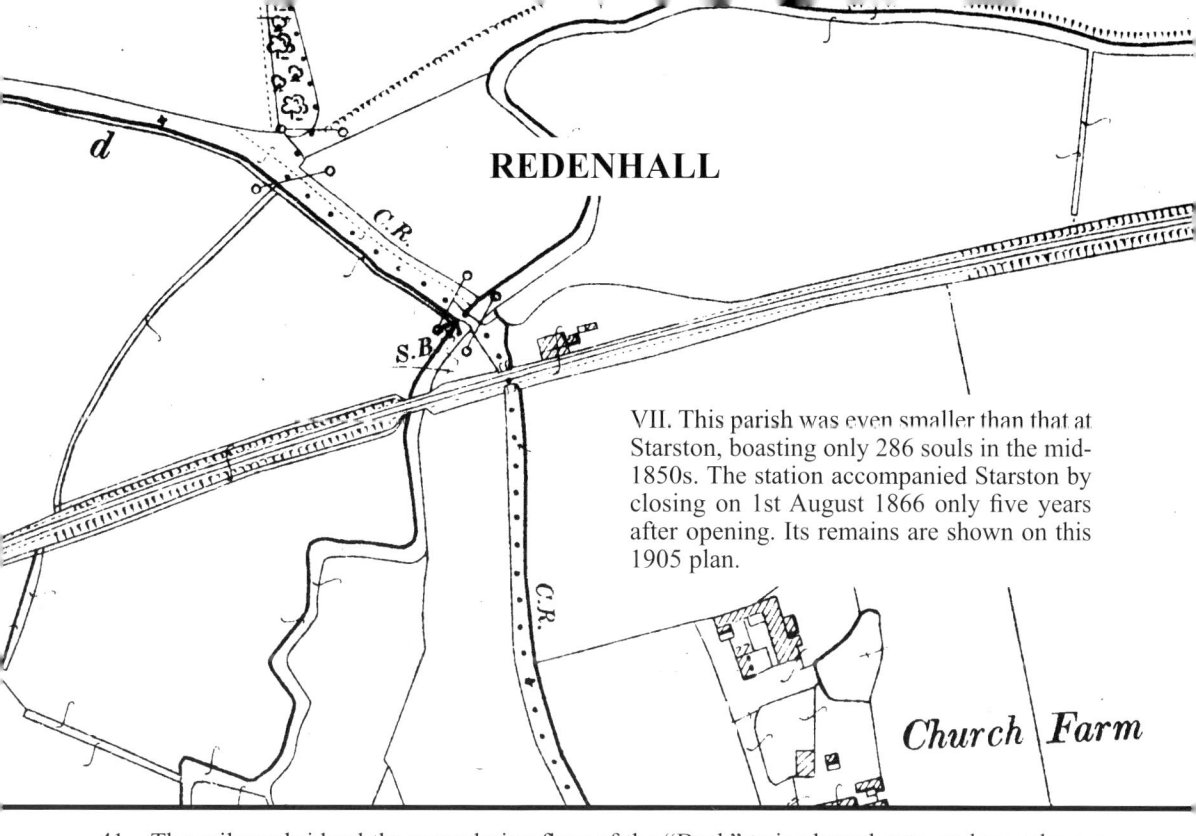

VII. This parish was even smaller than that at Starston, boasting only 286 souls in the mid-1850s. The station accompanied Starston by closing on 1st August 1866 only five years after opening. Its remains are shown on this 1905 plan.

41. The railway bridged the meandering flow of the "Beck" twice hereabouts, and we take our first look at the 1912 flood damage with this scene of destruction, looking west near Redenhall. (P.Standley collection)

42. This was another short-lived station, but as at Starston the building was still standing in the 1960s, a century after closure. (NRS Archive)

43. Now we are looking towards Harleston on the same day, and can see that the platform facing is still in place. A milepost and a fine crop of lupins are growing from the surface of the former platform. Even after the rails were lifted, the station house and canopy survived next to the overgrown trackbed until they were eventually swept away in connection with a road improvement scheme. (NRS Archive)

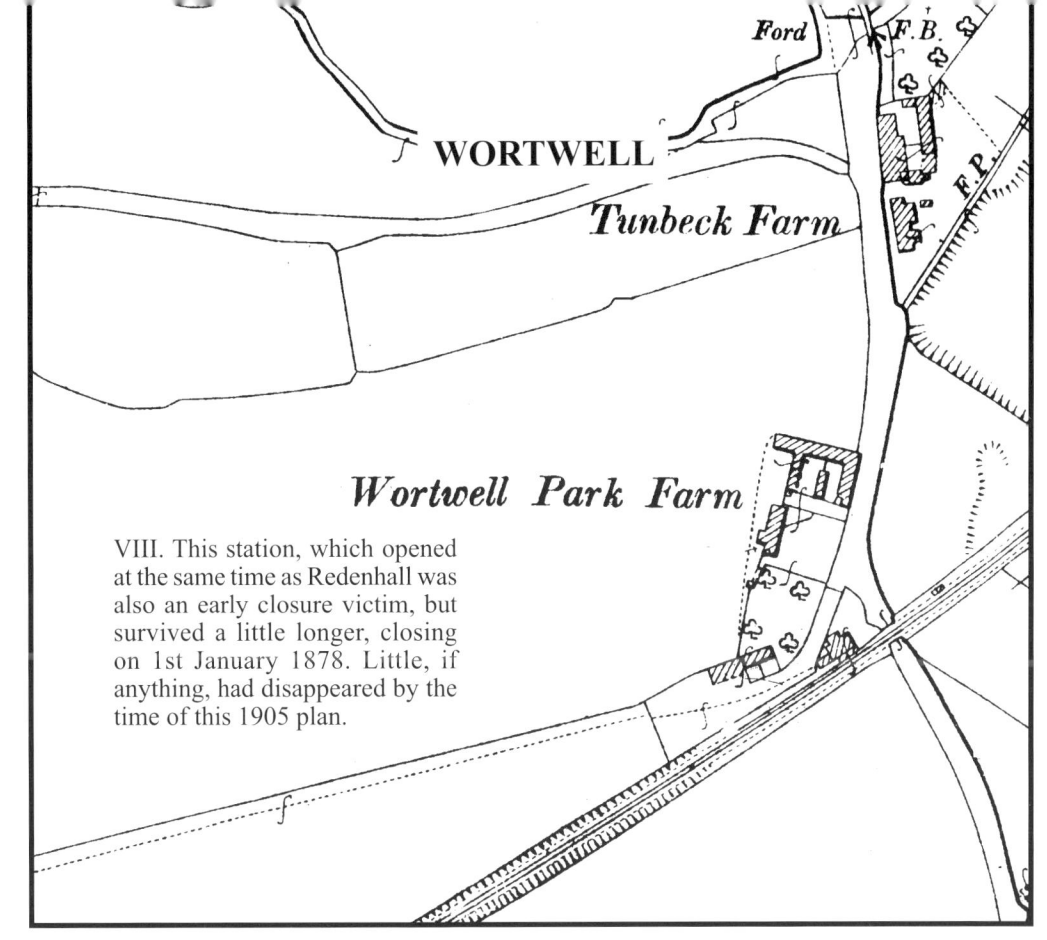

VIII. This station, which opened at the same time as Redenhall was also an early closure victim, but survived a little longer, closing on 1st January 1878. Little, if anything, had disappeared by the time of this 1905 plan.

44. Here too the station house, which had been enlarged with an extra bedroom at a cost of £55 in 1874, remained almost intact as the crossing keeper's accommodation, complete with canopy. We are looking east in 1951, and again the platform facing can be made out, although partially obscured by plant growth. (B.D.J.Walsh)

45. On a fine May morning in 1958, the photographer is enjoying a trip on the brake van of the Norwich to Bungay goods train, which has just crossed the minor road east of the station. The guard is closing the level crossing gates behind it, enabling a solitary cyclist to resume his journey. (B.Reading)

HOMERSFIELD

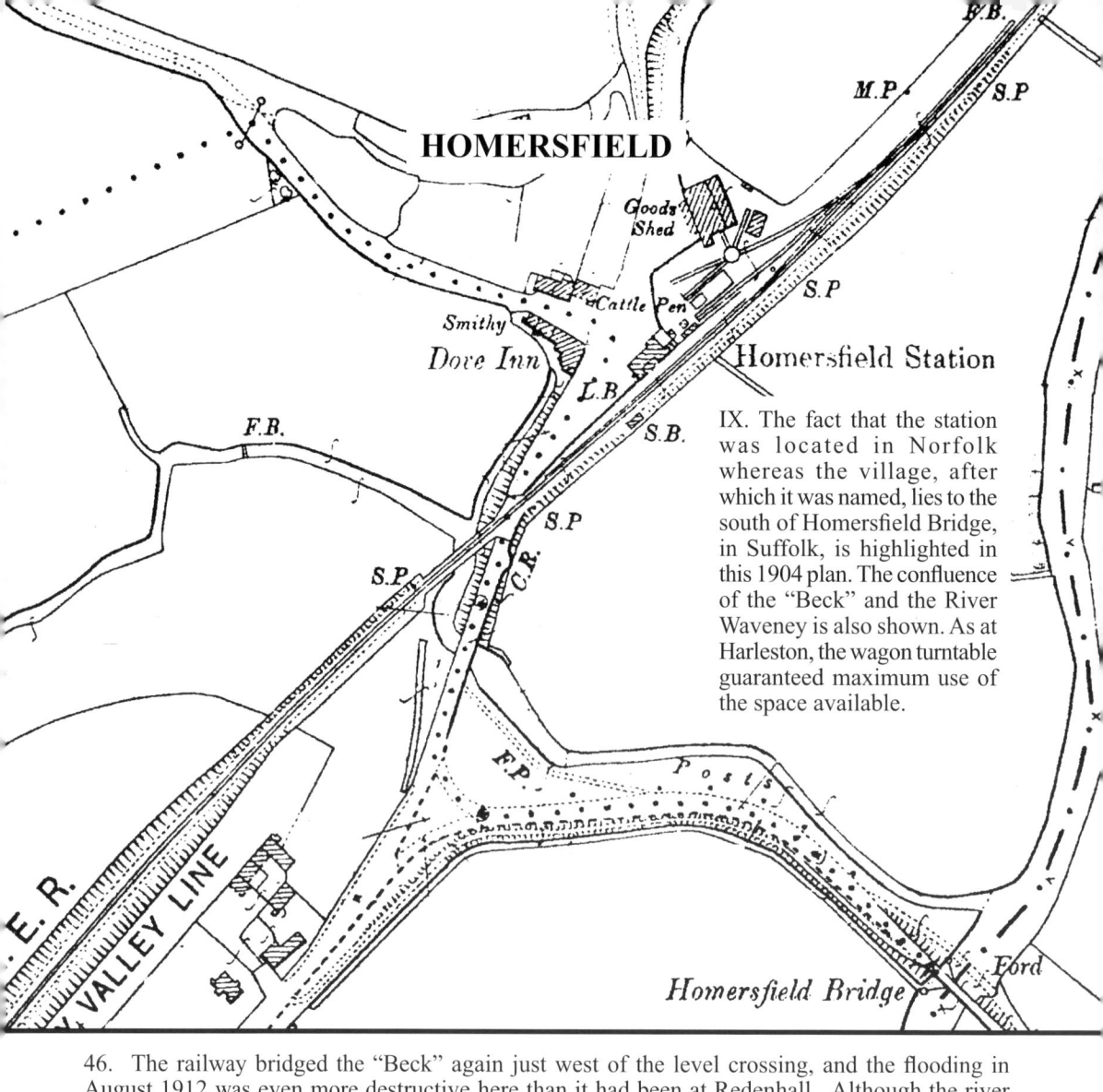

IX. The fact that the station was located in Norfolk whereas the village, after which it was named, lies to the south of Homersfield Bridge, in Suffolk, is highlighted in this 1904 plan. The confluence of the "Beck" and the River Waveney is also shown. As at Harleston, the wagon turntable guaranteed maximum use of the space available.

46. The railway bridged the "Beck" again just west of the level crossing, and the flooding in August 1912 was even more destructive here than it had been at Redenhall. Although the river bridge seems to have survived the deluge, the embankment has been undermined, and a signal post, securely lashed in place, overhangs the stream at a crazy angle. (P.Standley collection)

47. Now we look eastwards, from a point close to the level crossing, to find that the torrent has swept away both the roadway and the western section of the platform. Fencing and a fallen telegraph pole join the crossing gate in the general debris beside the sagging track.
(G.W.Gosling collection)

48. Following rebuilding, the bridge remained in the original trestle design, but the substantial replacement piers and abutments are prominent in this view from the south dated 16th May 1923. The stream that had caused all the trouble flows gently among the greenery.
(Bungay Museum/Frank Honeywood collection)

49. Horses are grazing in the meadows as a class J15 0-6-0 coasts into the deserted platform during 1944. This was the nearest station to Hardwick airfield, and many an American serviceman would find himself in the claustrophobic confines of a Liberator bomber in the flak-filled skies over Germany within hours of arriving at this peaceful spot. (J.W.Archer)

50. It is the Summer of 1951 and the flowers by the railings are in full bloom as the driver looks back before starting the next stage of his leisurely journey eastwards. Beyond the tall GER signal, there is just one van in the goods yard, but four months later the yard would be crammed with sugar beet traffic. (G.W.Powell)

51. A low Winter sun is beginning to disperse the mist, as we look eastwards from the level crossing, again in the early 1950s. The station and signal box look very neat and tidy, and a solid concrete platform facing has been provided to prevent a repetition of the 1912 damage. (Stations UK)

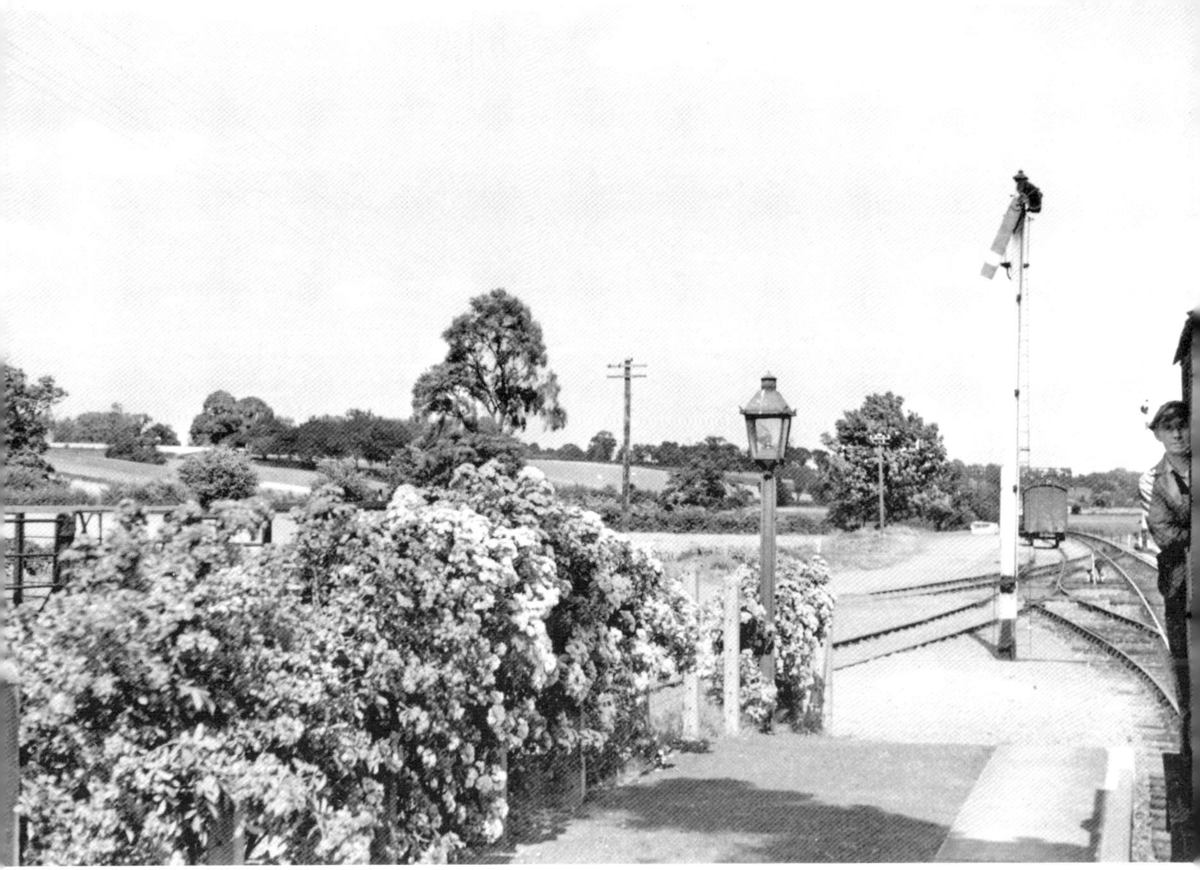

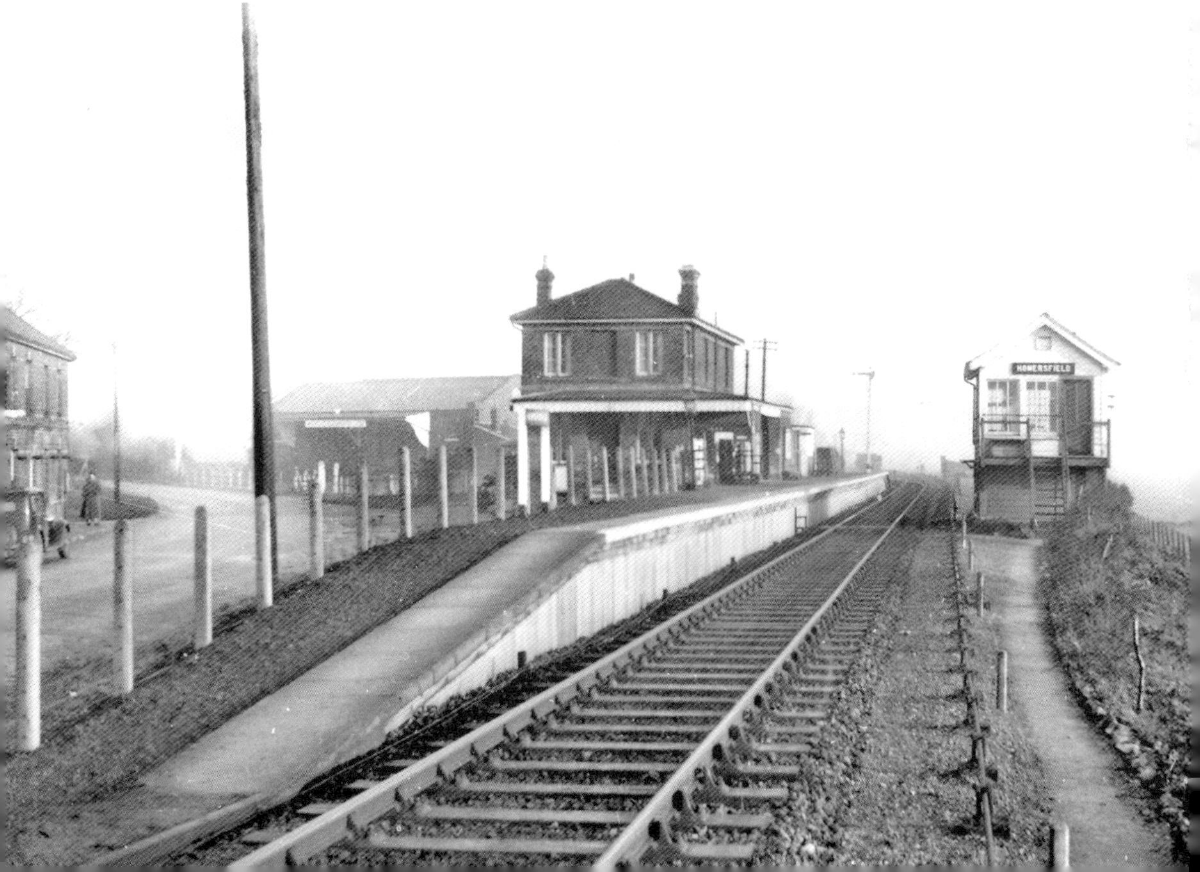
HOMERSFIELD

52. The peace of a Winter afternoon is disturbed briefly as a former GER 2-4-2T starts a train for Tivetshall during 1952. The starter signal is a modern upper quadrant, which contrasts with the Great Eastern relic at the other end of the station, shown in pictures 49 and 50. (Stations UK)

53. Class J15 0-6-0 no. 65469 makes a photo stop with the railtour on 8th October 1960. It is nearly 5 pm and the engine catches the last of the afternoon light as knots of people gather on the grassgrown tracks. In a few minutes time, the final train to travel over the whole of the line will be on its way again, heading for Beccles and the East Suffolk main line. (M.Fordham)

54. The photographer has parked his Ford Prefect in the station forecourt before recording the scene in October 1960. In 1958 the station had handled 1405 tons of inward traffic, mainly road stone chippings, fertiliser and wet pulp, and 1112 tons, mostly sugar beet, were despatched. However, this was not enough to prevent goods traffic from being withdrawn on 1st February 1960. The base of the signal box is on the right. (G.R.Siviour)

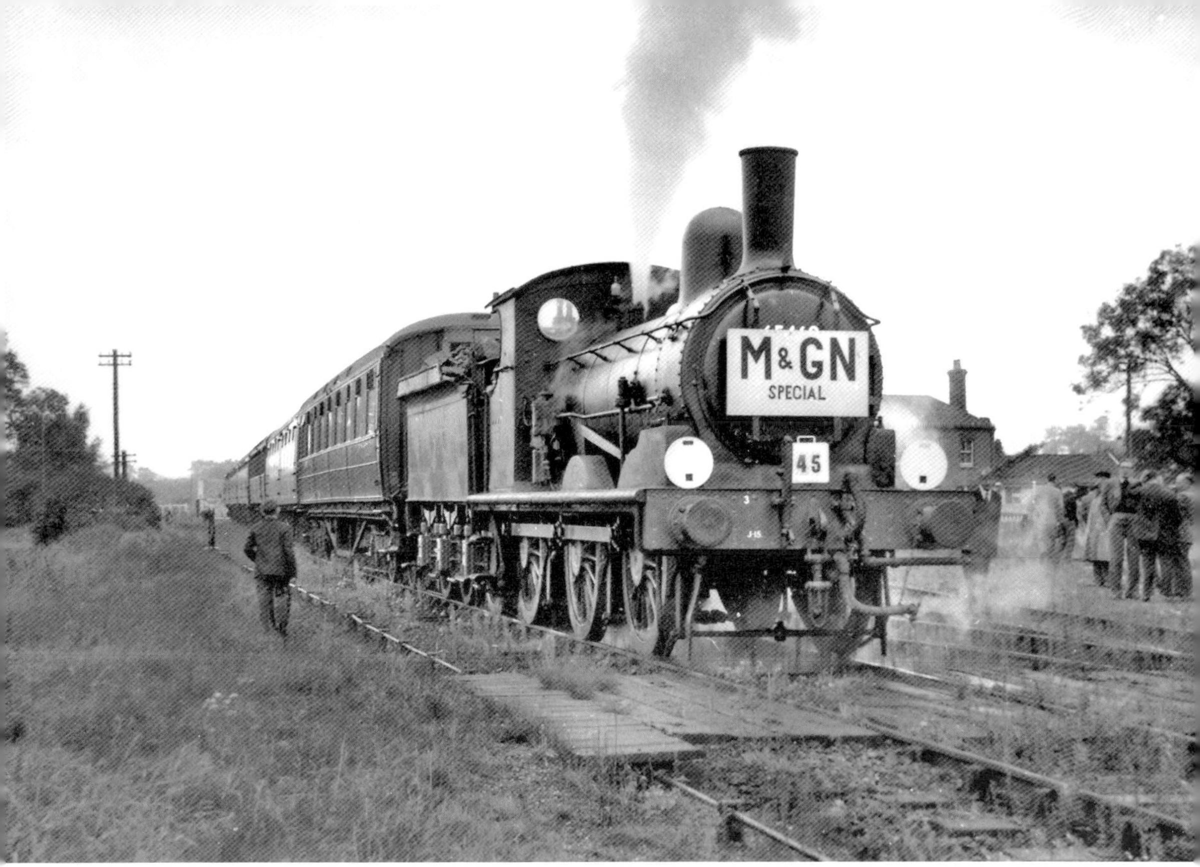
M&GN
SPECIAL
45

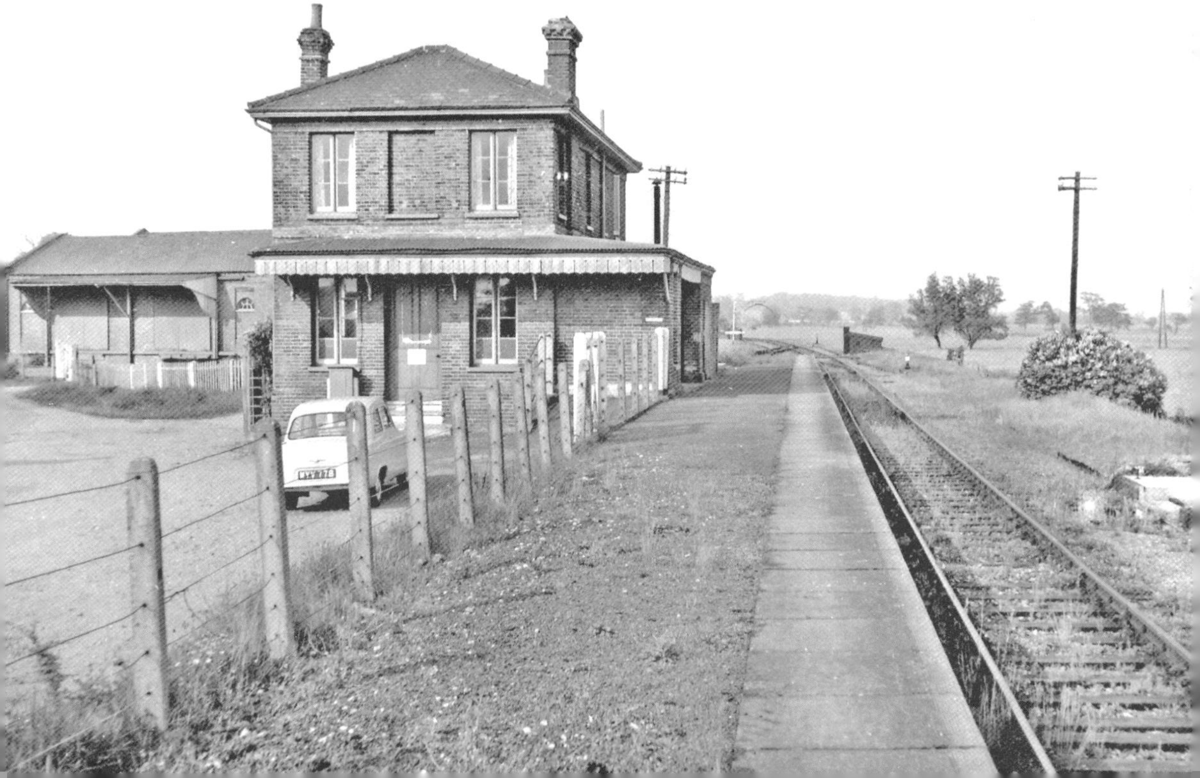

55. A glance at the plan will reveal that the wagon turntable was the focal point of the goods yard. The turntable, dating from 1860, was still in place in the disused yard in March 1961. The upper line on the left-hand side of the picture leads to the goods shed. (J.Watling)

56. We have seen the goods shed in the distance earlier. Here it is from the south on 24th May 1962, still intact although the tracks have been lifted. The building survived into 2004 as industrial premises, close to the A143 road, which follows the route of the railway between Bungay and Harleston. (J.Watling)

57. Finally, we leave the railway to look back at the goods shed and station building from the north east on 3rd July 1966. This picture emphasises the full extent of both buildings, the size of which is not apparent from more conventional viewpoints.
(Railway Record of the British Isles/G.L.Pring)

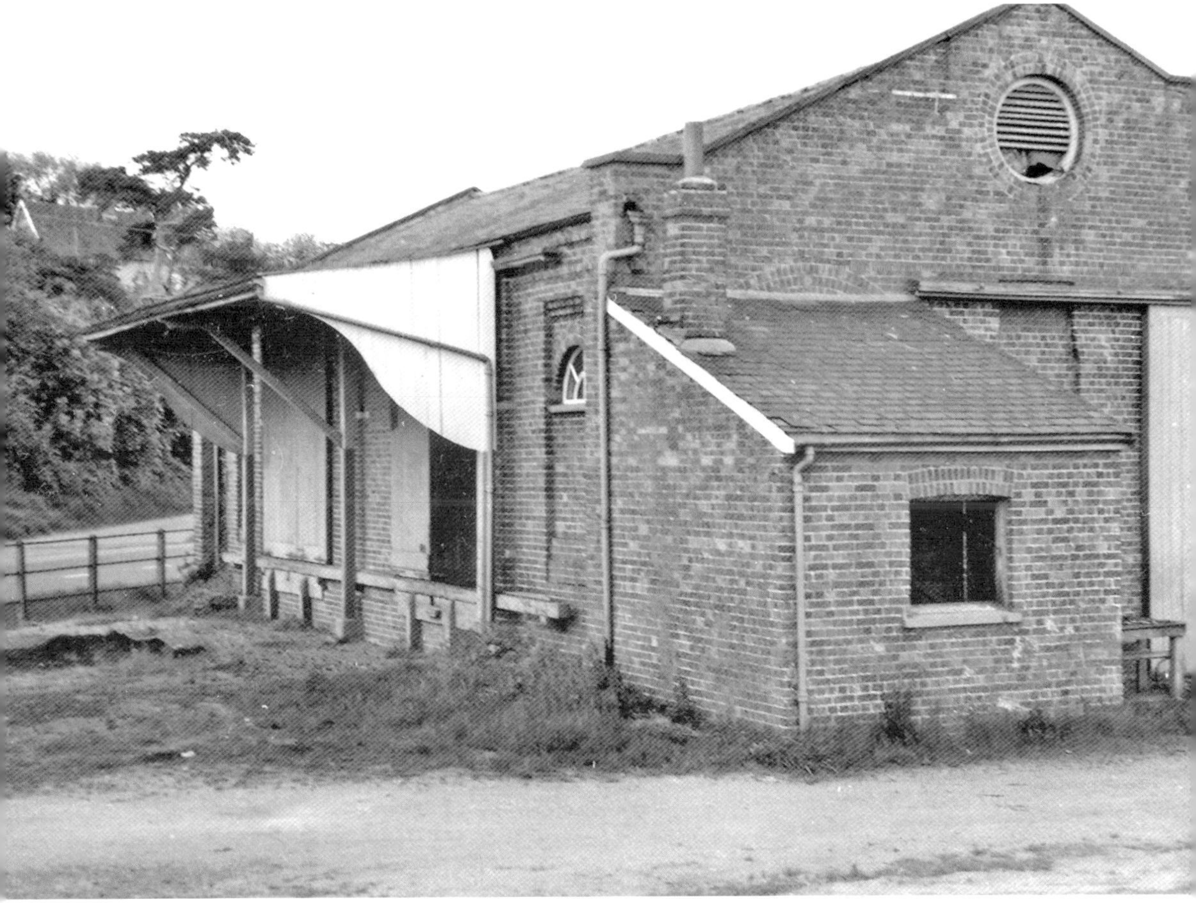

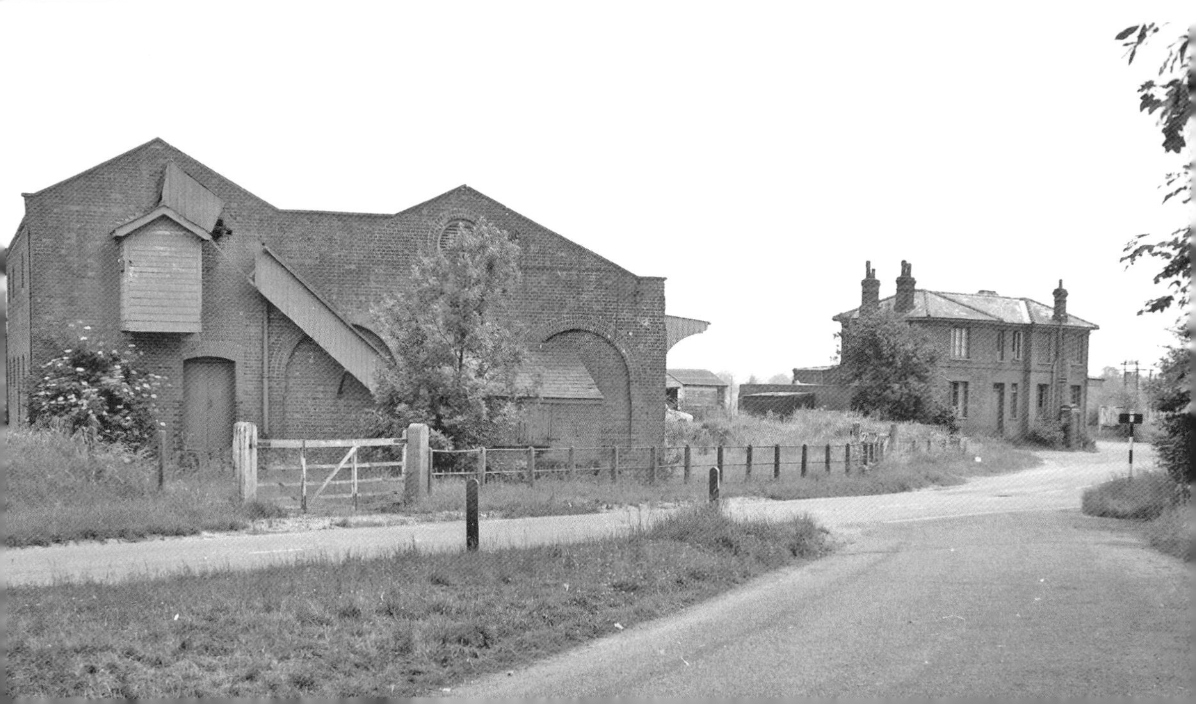

WEST OF EARSHAM

58. During World War II, a long double-ended siding was installed a mile or so to the west of Earsham station, in connection with the bomber offensive centred on nearby airfields. It was built to the north of the line, together with a substantial concrete loading area for road vehicles. Here we see a trainload of bombs being unloaded in 1944, with the running line on the right. It is recorded that 625 trains, comprising 21,038 wagons and carrying 200,000 tons of freight were handled here over a period of no more than three years, generating revenue of some £359,100. During peak times the loads were despatched directly to the airfields, and on other occasions were stored in the bomb dump on the nearby Earsham Hall Estate. After the war, the process was reversed, and unused bombs were taken away by rail for eventual dumping at sea. This traffic continued until 1954, and the disused siding was still in place in 1960 when this section of the line closed entirely. (J.W.Archer)

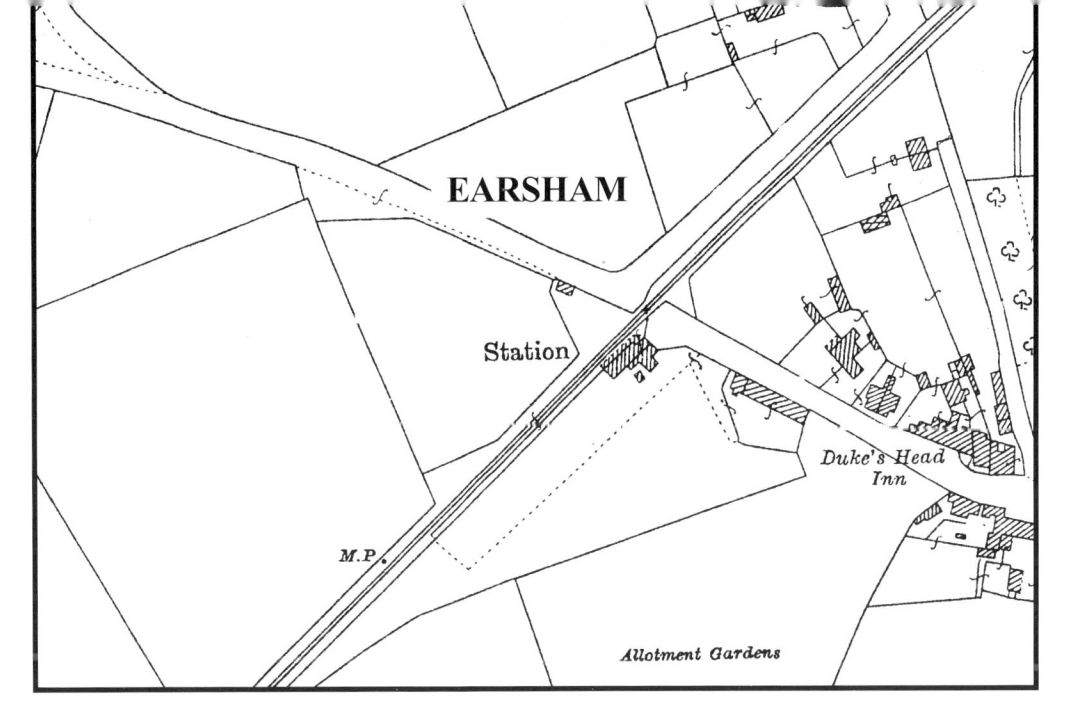

X. It would appear that sufficient land was purchased to the south of the line to accommodate a goods yard. In the event construction never took place and, of the original stations on the line, this location shared, with Starston, Redenhall and Wortwell, the distinction of having no siding accommodation. Unlike the others three, it managed to maintain its "open" status until the branch passenger service was withdrawn. However, it did suffer a temporary closure for just over three years as a result of economies during World War I. The plan dates from 1927.

59. The station and signal box are the first signs of habitation as we approach the village from the north, early in the twentieth century. For the first 25 years this must have been a very basic stopping place, as construction of the booking office and stationmasters house, at a cost of £350, was not authorised until 1884. (P.Standley collection)

60. Now we have reached the level crossing and look along Station Road towards the village. A few people have made their way into the picture, and the frock-coated railwayman, standing on the verandah of the signal box, is making sure that he doesn't miss out. (Bungay Museum/Frank Honeywood collection)

61. We move forward some fifty years to around 1950, to view the station and level crossing from the north-east. By now the signal box has been demolished, and a three-lever ground frame next to the crossing gate is an adequate replacement. (A.G.Forsyth/Initial Photographics)

62. There is no doubt about the location, as we look eastwards at much the same time. As at other locations along the line, a small enamel nameplate had replaced a far more substantial GER running in board during the LNER era. (Stations UK)

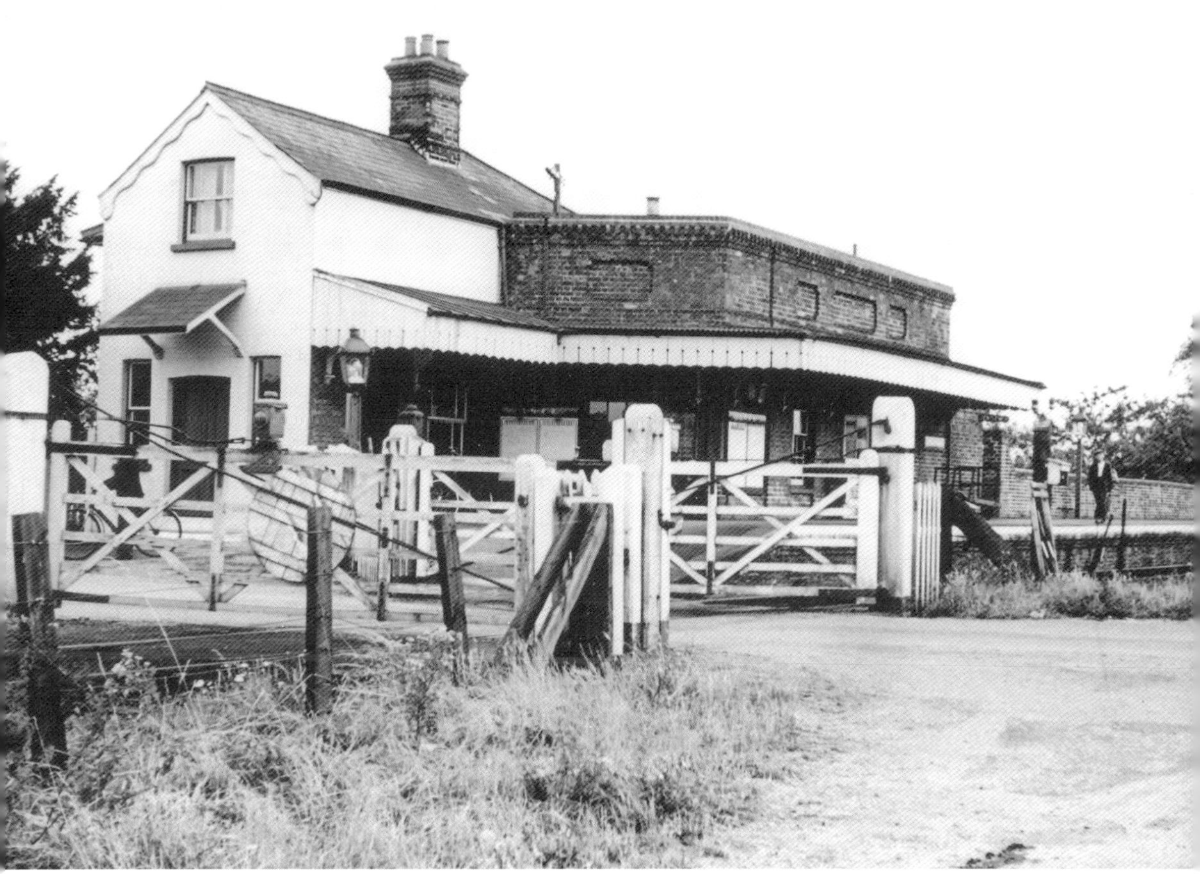

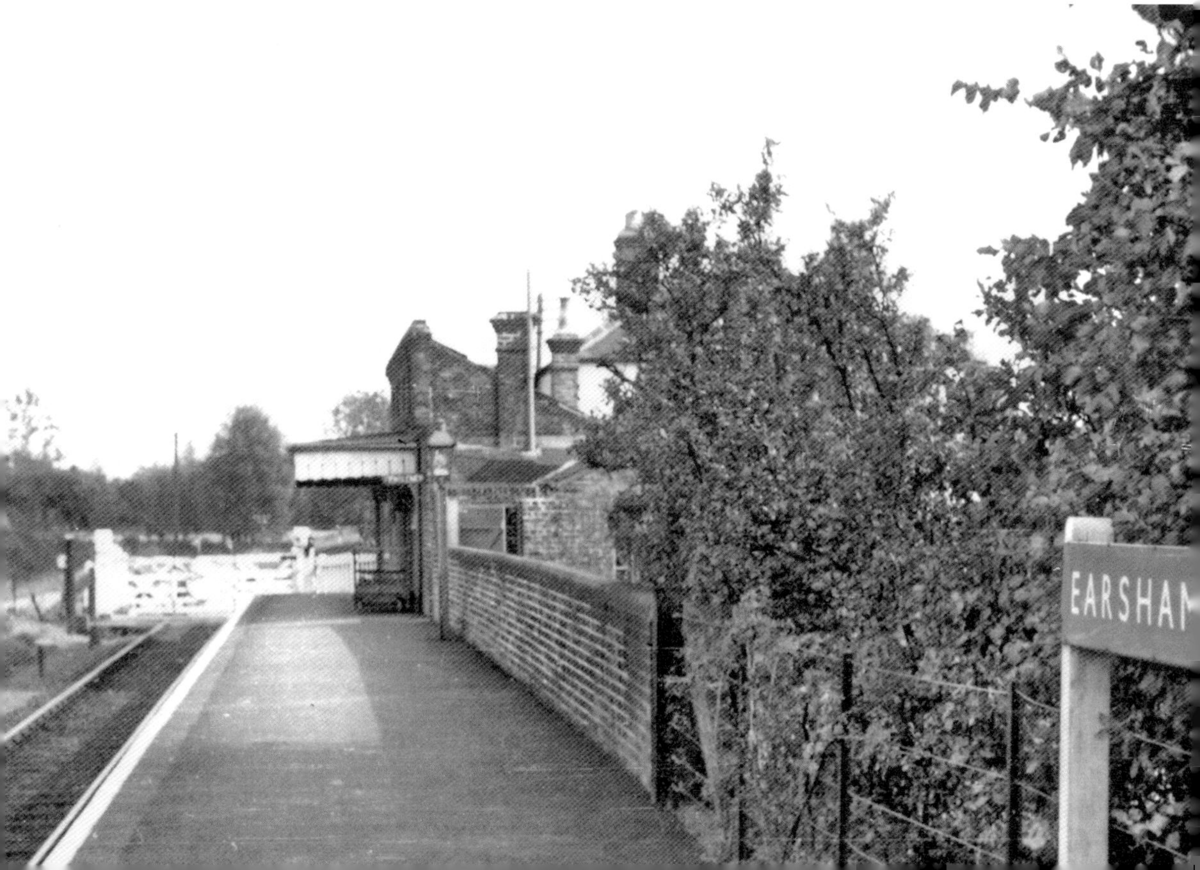
EARSHAM

63. Closure is not far off, as a railwayman makes his way along the snow-covered platform. In the absence of any goods facilities, the station closed entirely when passenger services were withdrawn. However, the Bungay stationmaster, who was responsible for all the branch stations east of here, lived in the station house between 1953 and 1956, as there was no accommodation at Bungay. (B.D.J.Walsh)

1903

64. Although the door leading on to the platform has been bricked up, many other features of the station remained in November 2001. The A143 road is only a few yards away to the right of the picture, whilst the boat suggests, perhaps, that the danger of flooding is still a very real one! (G.L.Kenworthy)

1913

XI. This was the only station on the branch located in Suffolk, and it served the largest centre of population. The relatively generous nature of its layout is demonstrated by this 1927 plan. The passenger station approach road and forecourt (where "Station" is superimposed) was not railway owned until 1926. Prior to this a rent, latterly £20 per annum, had been paid to the Fen Reeve of Bungay Common for its use.

65. The three-arch bridge carrying Outney Road across the railway to the common divided the passenger station from the goods yard. Framed in one of the arches, the goods yard fans out to the south of the running line in October 1911. This view would change little over the next 45 years. (HMRS/H.F.Hilton collection)

66. We have already seen GER bus F 2441 at Harleston, deputising for the trains in the aftermath of the 1912 floods. Here it is at the other end of its journey, flanked by another GER bus, registration F 1612, and two horse-drawn carriages from a disappearing age.
(Bungay Museum/Frank Honeywood collection)

67. The smaller of the two wooden buildings on the up platform is certainly showing its age on 2nd November 1922. We get the impression that the advertising boards are helping to hold the walls together, whilst the roof looks distinctly fragile!
(Bungay Museum/Frank Honeywood collection)

68. A down passenger train has just arrived, so the goods train will soon be able to start its journey westwards. This picture dates from around 1924, and there is still a horse-drawn carriage waiting in the forecourt. To the right of the station building, we can see the earlier water tower on the north side of the line. (Stations UK)

1934

69. Standing in a somewhat isolated position on the northern edge of the town, with the wide expanse of the Common beyond, the original station was not the most impressive of structures. We are looking along the wide approach road towards the single-storey wooden buildings around 1930. (Bungay Museum/Frank Honeywood collection)

70. At much the same time, the shadow of the up starter signal falls across the platform, showing that the line westwards is clear as a train approaches the station through the distant road bridge. Sacks of mail are piled on a barrow by the lamp in the foreground, ready to be loaded into the guards van when the train comes to a stand. A brick built structure replaced the old wooden buildings in 1933. (Stations UK)

71. The morning sun illuminates the signal box, as the 9 am train from Beccles approaches the station on 1st September 1951. Beyond the bridge, class F4 2-4-2T no. 67186 waits to continue its journey with the 8.35 am train from Tivetshall. During the latter years this meeting, at around 9.15 am, was the only occasion that two passenger trains were timetabled to pass each other here. Sometimes a van loaded with up to 1000 chips of mushrooms had to be moved manually from the goods yard on to the rear of the up train, adding to the workload of the four members of the station staff at this busy time. (H.C.Casserley)

72. Class B12 4-6-0 no. 61535 stands in the goods yard during the early months of 1952. Winter storms had caused considerable damage to trees in the area, and the engine had brought the steam crane from Ipswich depot to assist with loading the felled timber. A lighter rail-mounted crane, an M&GN vehicle still bearing the initials of its former owners, is to the left of the picture, and the jib of the heavy crane can be seen on the extreme right. Other large engines involved in this work included B12/3 no. 61577 and a D16/3 4-4-0. (Dr I.C.Allen/The Transport Treasury)

73. The station gardens are in bloom as class E4 2-4-0 no. 62789 pauses with a down train on a post-war Summer day. Together with the 2-4-2Ts and the J15s, these were the only locomotives normally seen east of Bungay, owing to weight restrictions. The front coach is a long way from the territory of its native Great Central Railway. (A.G.Forsyth/Initial Photographics)

74. Class F4 2-4-2T no. 67167 has arrived with a down train on 22nd July 1952. This time the coaches are considerably more modern corridor vehicles, so the train is probably the 8.35 am from Tivetshall, whose coaches formed a Lowestoft to Rugby train later in the day. The driver appears to be adopting a potentially painful contortion in an attempt to get some fresh air! (Mid-Rail Photographs)

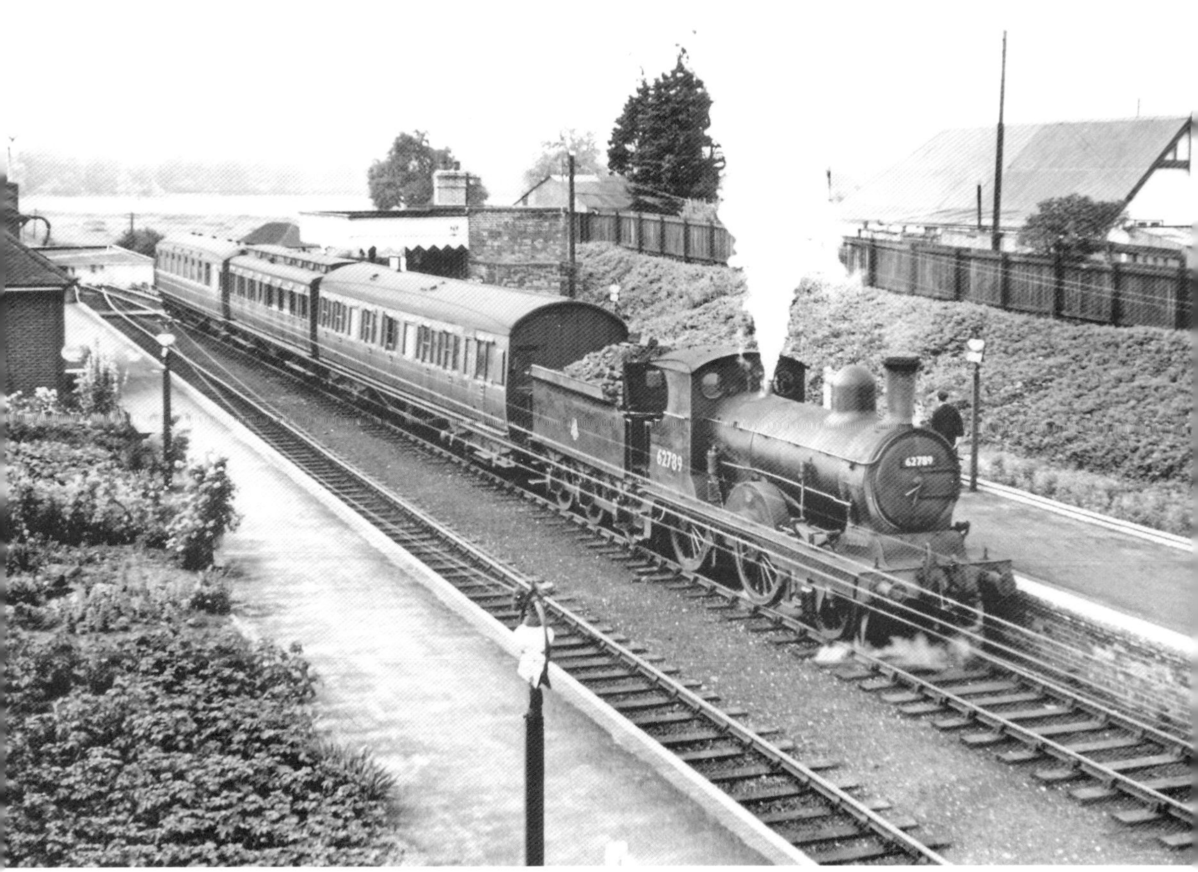
62789
62789

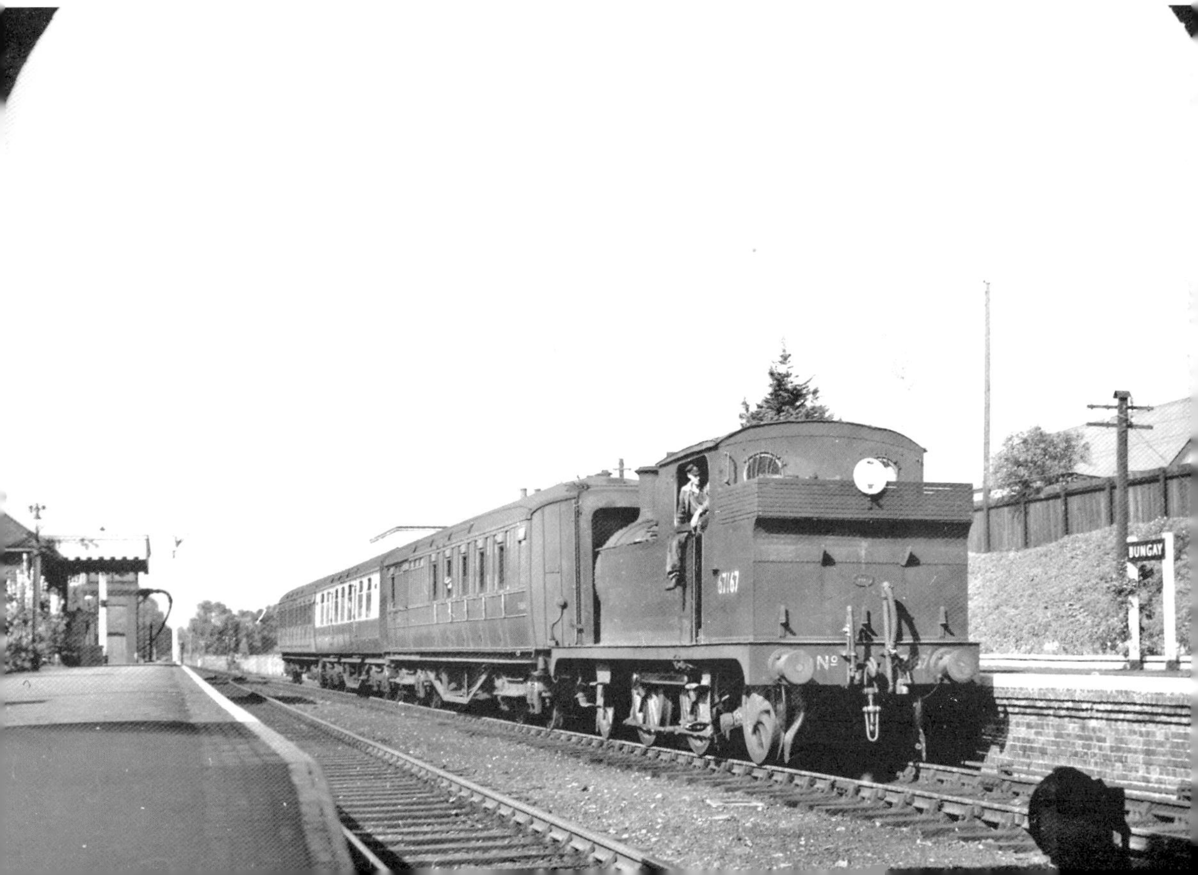
67167
BUNGAY

75. At much the same time, the signalman walks down the platform with the single-line token slung over his arm, closely followed by a 2-4-2T with a passenger train. Once the train has stopped there will be time for a gossip with the footplate crew as the tokens are exchanged. (B.D.J.Walsh)

76. Class E4 2-4-0 no. 62789 and a class J15 0-6-0 have pulled up beyond the end of the platform with a school special bound for London in 1952. The last four coaches are at the platform, enabling Bungay pupils to board the train, whilst some of their fellows from points further west are leaning excitedly out of the windows of the second coach, eagerly anticipating their day out. (T.Durrant)

77. We move indoors, for a rare look at the interior of the booking office. The ticket rack holds a wide variety of tickets for various destinations, and the window will be opened to the public well before the next train is due. A delightful jumble of papers, string, old ledgers and an ink bottle provides a reminder of office life in the early 1950s. (T.Durrant)

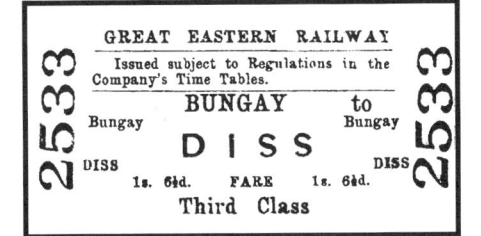

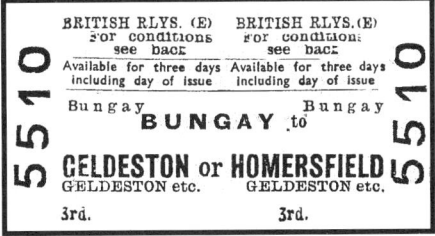

GREAT EASTERN RAILWAY	BRITISH RLYS. (E) / BRITISH RLYS. (E)
2533 — Issued subject to Regulations in the Company's Time Tables. **BUNGAY** to Bungay **DISS** DISS 1s. 6½d. FARE 1s. 6½d. Third Class — 2533	5510 — For conditions see back / For conditions see back. Available for three days including day of issue / Available for three days including day of issue. Bungay / Bungay **BUNGAY** to **GELDESTON or HOMERSFIELD** GELDESTON etc. / GELDESTON etc. 3rd. / 3rd. — 5510

78. Undeterred by an LNER sign threatening that "Trespassers will be prosecuted", the photographer has recorded the scene eastwards from just beyond the platform end during the final months of passenger services. The replacement water tower had been built on the south side of the line by 1931. (B.D.J.Walsh)

79. Between 1953 and 1960, the destinations of the daily goods trains varied. In 1954 trains from each direction terminated at Harleston; in 1956 there was a Norwich to Bungay working via Tivetshall, while the train from Beccles went no further than Ditchingham. Class J15 0-6-0 no. 65469 takes water after working the goods from Norwich on a May morning in 1958. (B.Reading)

80. A class J15 stands in the station with a goods train during the 1950s. The overgrown station garden testifies to the absence of passenger trains, and the redundant brick waiting room on the down platform has been demolished. (Dr I.C.Allen/The Transport Treasury)

81. The exterior of the 1933 building was plain and functional, but looked considerably more substantial than its predecessor. It was at its busiest between 1942 and 1945 as the railhead for the airfields, and on occasions the daily takings exceeded £500. As we see here, the building remained in use after the passenger closure, but it had been demolished by the mid-1970s.
(J.Watling collection)

82. Beyond the goods yard, the line narrowed to single track over a level crossing. With the crossing keepers hut, signals, and well-tended track there is little to indicate that this picture was taken as late as the 1960s. (NRS Archive)

83. Goods services were withdrawn on 3rd August 1964. In September 1965 weeds are growing on the one remaining track, which terminates in buffer stops at the platform end. Beyond the water tower, the empty trackbed stretches across the meadows towards Earsham. (J. Watling)

1943

Miles from Tivetshall		mrn	mrn	mrn	aft	aft		Miles from Beccles		mrn	mrn	mrn	aft	aft	aft	
	3 London (L'poolSt. dep	..	8 12	10 0	1 04	0	..		3 London (L'poolSt dep	..	4 40	8 12	12 20	3 40	4 0	..
	3 Norwich (Thorpe)	7 0	11 5	1 10	4 55	7 20	..		3 Yarmouth (S.T.)	..	8 15	8 55	2 40	9 10	7 0	..
	3 Forncett	7 24	1 29	1 34	5 19	7 45	..		3 Lowestoft (C.)	..	..	5 11	5	2 48	6 10	7 10
	Tivetshall dep	7 41	1 40	1 55	5 29	7 55	..		Beccles dep	5 35	9 0	12 35	3 50	6 35	8 6	..
2½	Pulham Market	7 40	1 46	2 1	5 35	8 1	..	2½	Geldeston	..	9 6	12 41	..	3 56	6 41	8 12	..
3½	Pulham St. Mary	7 43	1 49	2 4	5 38	8 4	..	4½	Ellingham	..	9 10	12 45	..	3 40	6 45	8 16	..
6½	Harleston	7 49	1 56	2 13	5 44	8 11	..	5½	Ditchingham	5 49	9 14	12 49	..	3 44	6 49	8 20	..
9	Homersfield	7 55	12 2	2 19	5 50	8 17	..	6½	Bungay	5 54	9 19	12 55	..	3 49	6 53	8 26	..
12	Earsham	8 1	12 8	2 25	5 56	8 23	..	7½	Earsham	..	9 22	12 58	..	3 52	6 56	8 29	..
13	Bungay	8 5	12 12	2 32	6 0	8 27	..	10½	Homersfield	6 4	9 29	1 5	..	3 59	7 3	8 36	..
13¾	Ditchingham	8 9	12 16	2 36	6 4	8 30	..	13½	Harleston	6 11	9 35	1 11	..	4 5	7 10	8 42	..
15½	Ellingham	8 13	12 20	2 40	6 8	8 34	..	15½	Pulham St. Mary	6 17	9 41	1 17	..	4 11	7 16	8 48	..
16½	Geldeston	8 17	12 24	2 44	6 12	8 38	..	16½	Pulham Market	6 20	9 44	1 20	..	4 14	7 19	8 51	..
19½	Beccles arr	8 24	12 30	2 50	6 18	8 44	..	19½	Tivetshall arr	6 26	9 50	1 26	..	4 20	7 25	8 57	..
28	3 Lowestoft (C.) arr	8 50	2 15	4 35	6 52	9 12	..	23	3 Forncett arr	6 37	10 0	1 45	..	4 29	7 38	9 6	..
32	3 Yarmouth (S.T.)	9 12	2 63	3 20	6 52	9 20	..	34	3 Norwich (Thorpe)	7 0	10 25	2 10	..	4 52	8 11	9 29	..
128¾	3 London (L'poolSt.)	11 36	3 57	6 51	10 15	..	..	120	3 London (L'poolSt.)	10 45	1 35	5 0	..	7 14	11 25	12 45	..

A Via Norwich. B Arr. 3 35 aft on Sats. L One class only, except on Sats. S Sats. only. X One class only.
Y Arr 7 10 aft on Sats

84. With the signalbox base on the left, the abandoned goods yard awaits the demolition men on 25th September 1965. A much-needed bypass for the town was opened in November 1983, using the alignment of the old railway between Ditchingham and Earsham. (J.Watling)

G. E. R.

Bungay

85. A crane is lifting the long-disused water tank from the brick tower, before loading it on to a lorry, bound for Weybourne on the North Norfolk Railway. The largest surviving relic of the town's railway continued to serve its original purpose into the 21st Century, albeit some 35 miles to the north. (M&GN Archive Centre Trust)

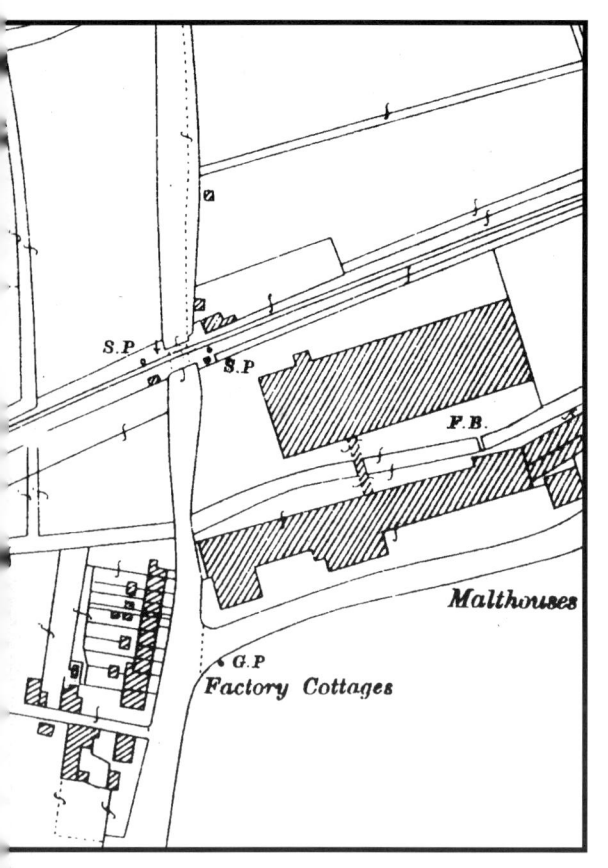

WEST OF DITCHINGHAM

XIIa. This plan, dating from 1927, shows the immediate vicinity of the Norwich Road level crossing. In 1943 the War Department took over the malthouses to the east of the crossing as a depot for the US Army and sidings were laid in to serve the premises; by the time of the Railway Inspector's post-war report in 1948, they had been removed. However, his visit was not totally wasted as the westward extension of the loop on the north side of the single line, also laid in 1943, was, according to the local staff, still in daily use.

86. Further flooding devastated the area in the late 1930s. We are west of the level crossing, known locally as Silk Factory Crossing, with the maltings to the right. Following flood damage on 26th January 1939, the Bungay stationmaster told the local newspaper that this section of line was "not safe to walk over, let alone send a train over." On the same day, a replacement bus ran into trouble hereabouts, and had to be towed to safety by a lorry. (Bungay Museum/Frank Honeywood collection)

87. A railwayman operates the ground frame next to the level crossing gate, as no. D2559 runs round its train in 1965. This ground frame controlled the western access to the loop, which connected with the goods yard at Ditchingham station. (Dr I.C.Allen/The Transport Treasury)

88. For some time after the official closure date, the line from Ditchingham to Beccles continued to handle regular block loads of sand, quarried near here. The duration of this traffic flow is uncertain, but there is evidence to suggest it lasted until August 1965. A Hunslet shunter stands on the wartime loop with this train. The extent of the loop is well illustrated – the chimney pots of the station are far away beyond the train, but the loco has not yet reached the east end of the maltings.
(Dr I.C.Allen/The Transport Treasury)

89. Close to the former level crossing, the shadow of the maltings complex falls across the course of the railway on 15th March 1981. The coach body seen in picture 88, a 6-wheeler built in 1895 and once providing 1st class, 3rd class and luggage accommodation, is beginning to show signs of old age. (Bungay Museum/Frank Honeywood collection/S.Leahy)

90. The maltings dwarf the crossing house, as we look eastwards along the trackbed towards Norwich Road on the same day. The route of the railway is still easy to trace, but would disappear under road improvements in the next year or so.
(Bungay Museum/Frank Honeywood collection/S.Leahy)

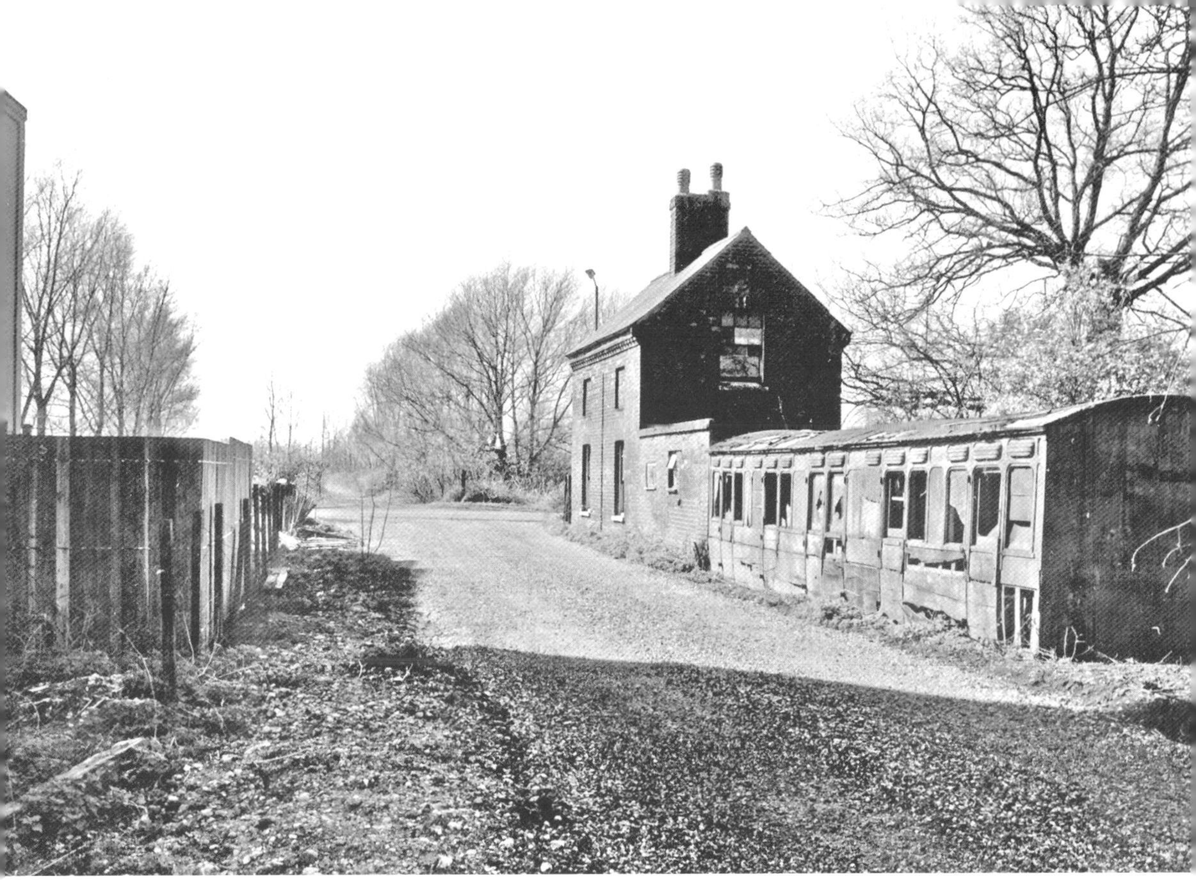

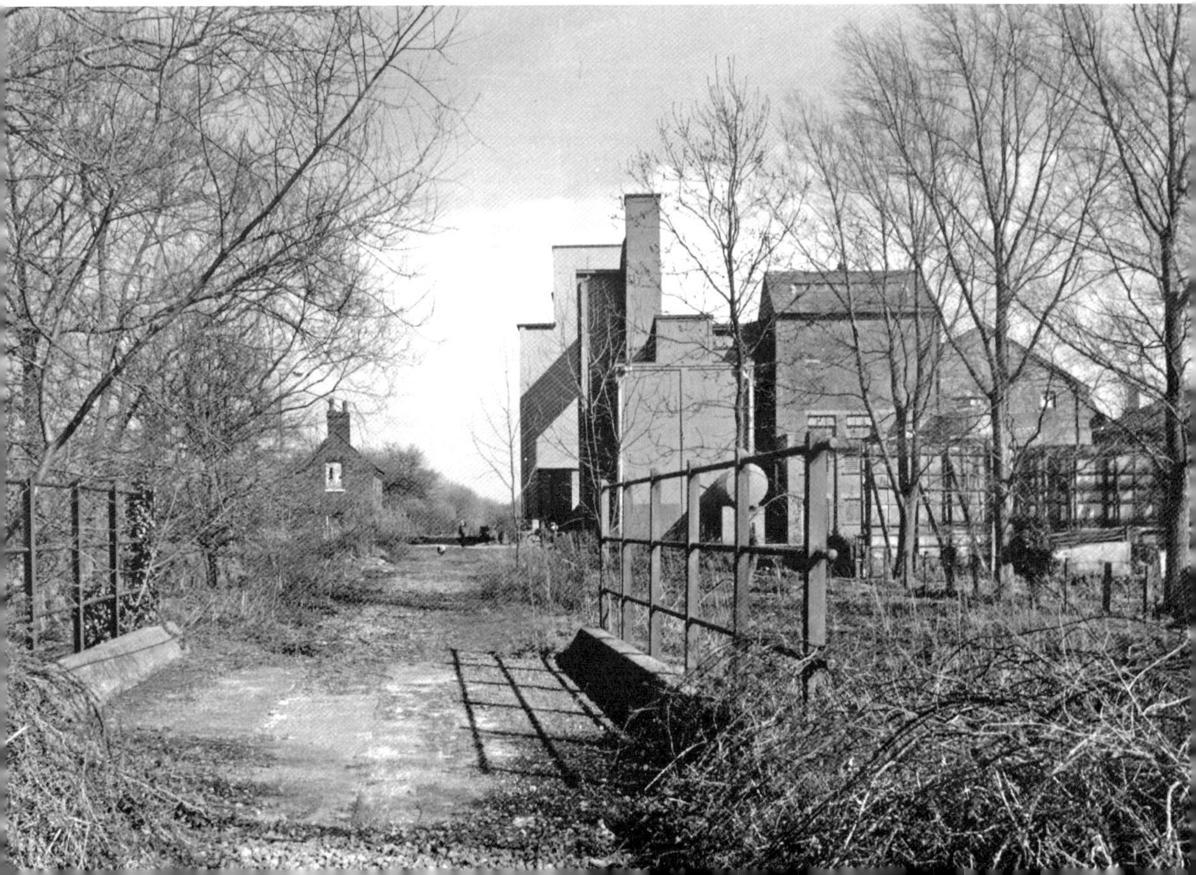

DITCHINGHAM

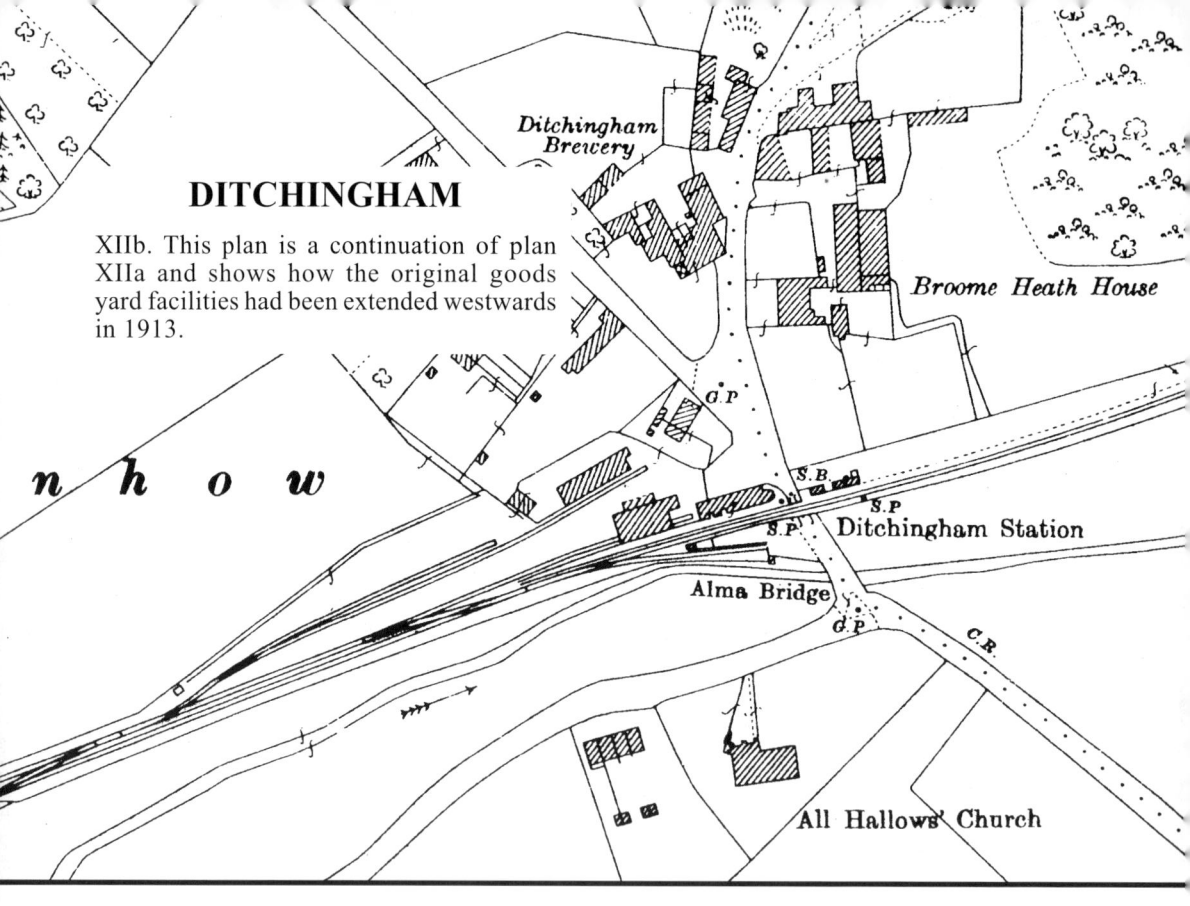

XIIb. This plan is a continuation of plan XIIa and shows how the original goods yard facilities had been extended westwards in 1913.

91. An early picture postcard shows the original extent of the station buildings, but the mature ivy growth suggests they are far from new. As with so many of these cards, the scene is full of human interest, although we do not know who the dignified pipe smoker is, nor why he is taking centre stage compared with the signalman and the three village lads. (P.Standley collection)

92. Some years later, a slightly different viewpoint allows us a view of the signal box, to the right of the muddy road surface. There are still plenty of people to enliven the scene, but the ivy has gone, making way for a new booking office and waiting room to the east of the main station building. This single-storey extension was authorised in 1912 at a cost of £172, and was in use by the end of 1913. (P.Standley collection)

G. E. R.

Ditchingham

93. Since leaving Starston, we have seen a variety of styles in the station architecture. For the remainder of the journey to Beccles though, the stations are similar to those west of Harleston. A good crowd has gathered in front of the familiar building, as their train approaches on a sunny day in 1950. (Stations UK)

1947

TIVETSHALL, BUNGAY, and BECCLES

Miles from Tivetshall	Week Days only	a.m	a.m	a.m W	p.m	p.m
	3 London (L'pool St.) dep	..	8 12	1025	1 0	5 6
	3 Norwich (Thorpe)	6 55	10 53	1 10	5 0	7 20
	3 Forncett .... "	6 57	11 17	1 34	5 24	7 46
	Tivetshall .... dep	7 19	11 25	2 0	5 32	8 15
2¾	Pulham Market	7 25	11 31	2 6	5 38	8 21
3¾	Pulham St. Mary	7 28	11 34	2 9	5 41	8 24
6½	Harleston	7 35	11 41	2 17	5 47	8 36
9	Homersfield	7 41	11 47	2 23	5 53	8 42
12	Earsham	7 47	11 53	2 29	5 59	8 48
13	Bungay	7 52	11 57	2 36	6 3	8 52
13¾	Ditchingham	7 57	12 1	2 41	6 7	8 56
15¼	Ellingham	8 1	12 5	2 45	6 11	9 0
16¾	Geldeston	8 5	12 9	2 49	6 15	9 4
19½	Beccles .... arr	8 11	12 15	2 55	6 23	9 10
28	3 Lowestoft (C.) .. arr	8 53	12 59	3 39	7 16	9 35
32	3 Yarmouth (S.T.). "	9 4	1X12	4V45	7 13	9X45
128¾	3 London (L'pool St.) "	11 28	3 37	..	10 22	..

Miles from Beccles	Week Days only	a.m	a.m W	a.m	p.m	p.m
	3 London (L'pool St) dep	4 25	..	10z25	3 44	4 0
	3 Yarmouth (S.T.) "	8X10	11 55	2 40	6 24	7 0
	3 Lowestoft (C.) ... "	7 58	11 53	2 38	5 20	7 12
—	Beccles .... dep	9 0	12 35	3 25	6 56	8 0
2¾	Geldeston	9 6	12 41	3 31	7 2	8 6
4¼	Ellingham	9 10	12 45	3 35	7 6	8 10
5¾	Ditchingham	9 14	12 49	3 39	7 10	8 14
6½	Bungay	9 19	12 55	3 44	7 15	8 20
7½	Earsham	9 22	12 58	3 47	7 18	8 23
10½	Homersfield	9 29	1 5	3 54	7 25	8 30
13½	Harleston	9 35	1 12	4 1	7 34	8 40
15¾	Pulham St. Mary	9 41	1 18	4 7	7 40	8 46
16¾	Pulham Market	9 44	1 21	4 10	7 43	8 49
19½	Tivetshall .... arr	9 50	1 27	4 15	7 49	8 55
23	3 Forncett .... arr	9 59	1 51	4 33	8 56	9 3
34	3 Norwich (Thorpe)	1016	2 21	4 58	8 20	9 31
120	3 London (L'pool St.) "	1 38	5 10	7 11	1230	2A30

A Via Norwich and Ely. S Saturdays only. V One class only. Arr. 3 39 p.m. on Saturdays (First and Third class)
W Wednesdays and Saturdays. X One class only. z Dep. 12 25 p.m. on Saturdays.

94. Here is the west end of the substantial brick built goods shed, together with the 1½ ton crane and a road trailer waiting in the yard. The 9 am train from Beccles is pulling away from the station on 1st September 1951. (H.C.Casserley)

1952

TIVETSHALL, BUNGAY, and BECCLES

Week Days only

Miles from Tivetshall		a.m	a.m	a.m	a.m	p.m	p.m	
	3 London (L'pool St.) dep	..	4 30	8 30	11 30	1 30	5 30	..
	3 Norwich (Thorpe) "	6 55	7 55	10 54	12 55	5 3	7 23	..
	3 Forncett "	6 57	8 19	11 18	1 19	5 27	7 49	..
—	Tivetshall dep	7 19	8 35	11 25	2 15	5 36	8 15	..
2½	Pulham Market	7 25	8 41	11 31	2 21	5 42	8 21	..
3½	Pulham St. Mary	7 28	8 44	11 34	2 24	5 45	8 24	..
6½	Harleston	7 36	8 56	11 41	2 32	5 51	8 35	..
9	Homersfield	7 42	9 2	11 47	2 38	5 57	8 42	..
12	Earsham	7 48	9 8	11 53	2 44	6 3	8 48	..
13	Bungay	7 52	9D20	11 56	2 47	6 7	8 51	..
13½	Ditchingham	7 57	9 24	12 0	2 51	6 11	8 55	A a.m. Via Norwich (Thorpe) and Ely
15	Ellingham	8 1	9 28	12 4	2 55	6 15	8 59	a a.m.
16½	Geldeston	8 5	9 32	12 8	2 59	6 19	9 3	B Arr. 1 16 p.m. on Mons., Fris. and Sats.
19½	Beccles arr	8 11	9 38	12 14	3 5	6 25	9 9	D Arr. 9 10 a.m.
28	3 Lowestoft (C.) arr	8 53	10 10	12 59	3 42	7 16	9 46	H Arr. 4 20 p.m. on Fridays and 4 16 p.m. on Saturdays
32	3 Yarmouth (S.T.) "	8 45	10 12	1 12	4J45	7 20	9 45	K Dep. 12 5 p.m. on Saturdays
128½	3 London (L'pool St.) "	11J34	11 30	3t56	..	6 48	9 46	L Arr. 1 20 p.m. on Saturdays

Week Days only

Miles from Beccles		a.m	a.m	a.m	p.m	p.m	p.m	S Saturdays only
	3 London (L'pool St.) dep	..	4 30	9S33	12S33	3 33	4 30	U From 25th July to 6th September arr. 11 30 a.m. on Fridays and 11 27 a.m. on Saturdays
	3 Yarmouth (S.T.) "	6 35	8 20	12 10	2 55	6 20	7 20	
	3 Lowestoft (C.) "	6 36	8 20	12K10	2 55	6 20	7 31	
—	Beccles dep	7 0	9 0	12 35	3 25	6 55	8 2	Z Arr. 3 41 p.m. on Saturdays
2½	Geldeston	7 6	9 6	12 41	3 31	7 1	8 8	‡ Arr. 3 11 p.m. on Saturdays
4½	Ellingham	7 10	9 10	12 45	3 35	7 5	8 12	
5½	Ditchingham	7 14	9 14	12 49	3 39	7 9	8 16	
6½	Bungay	7 19	9 19	12 53	3 44	7 13	8 20	
7½	Earsham	7 22	9 22	12 56	3 47	7 16	8 23	
10½	Homersfield	7 29	9 29	1 3	3 54	7 23	8 30	
13	Harleston	7 35	9 35	1 9	4 1	7 30	8 40	
15½	Pulham St. Mary	7 41	9 41	1 15	4 7	7 36	8 46	
16½	Pulham Market	7 44	9 44	1 18	4 10	7 39	8 49	
19½	Tivetshall arr	7 50	9 50	1 24	4 18	7 45	8 55	
22	3 Forncett	8 5	9 59	1 41	4 30	..	9 7	
54	3 Norwich (Thorpe) "	8 30	10 16	2 4	4 53	8 29	9 30	
120	3 London (L'pool St.) "	11 18	11 30	4K34	7 45	12 a 7	2J33	

95. The photographer has made his way to the cattle dock in order to record the view eastwards, with the line curving away across the wintry landscape past the signal box. Outside the waiting room, the platform has been cleared of snow, but this little courtesy will soon be irrelevant, as closure is imminent. (B.D.J.Walsh)

96. A class J15 0-6-0 passes the cattle dock as it arrives with an up passenger train on the same day. Despite the winter sunshine, it is bitterly cold on the footplate as the loco runs tender first through the countryside, and a tarpaulin has been hung across the back of the cab to offer the crew some protection from the elements. (B.D.J.Walsh)

97. Previous pictures have revealed three enamel signs facing on to the platform and proclaiming the station name. All have now gone, together with the seats and lamps, and although everything is neat and tidy, we can be in no doubt that this view dates from after 1953. This station, too, was the victim of a road improvement scheme, being demolished in October 1982.
(The Lens of Sutton collection)

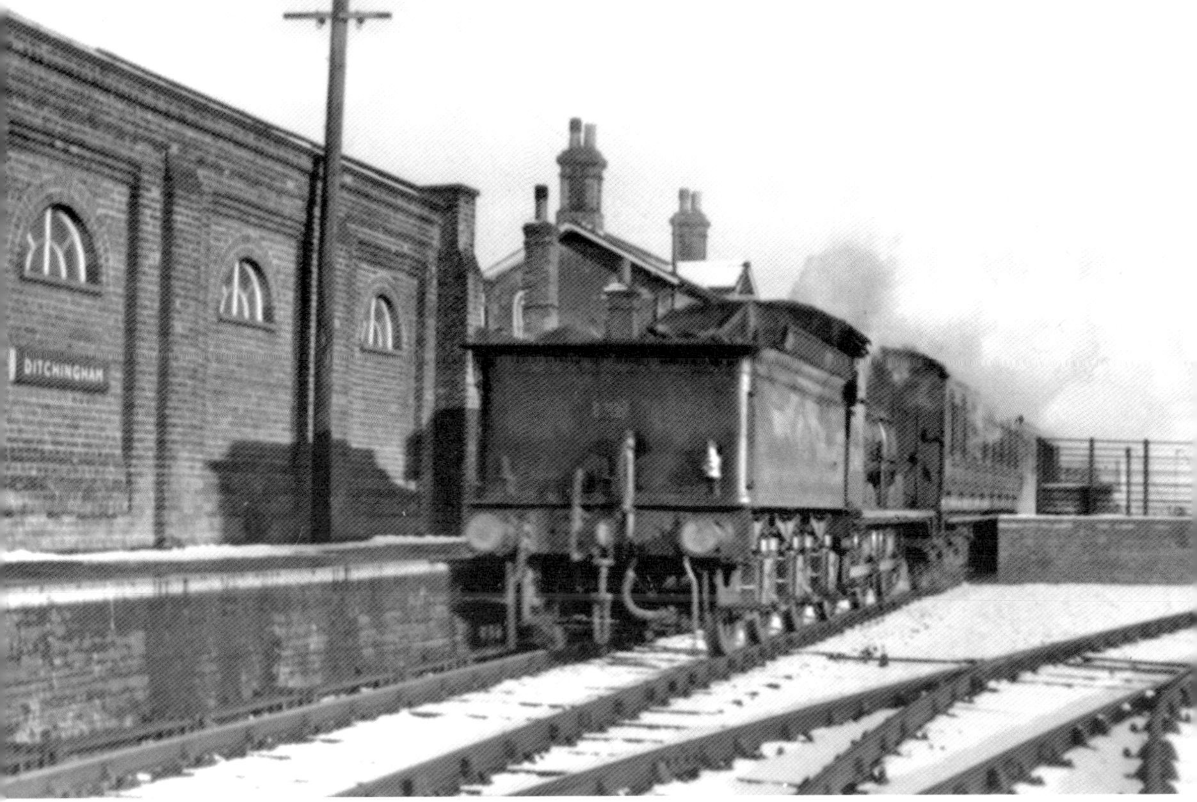
DITCHINGHAM

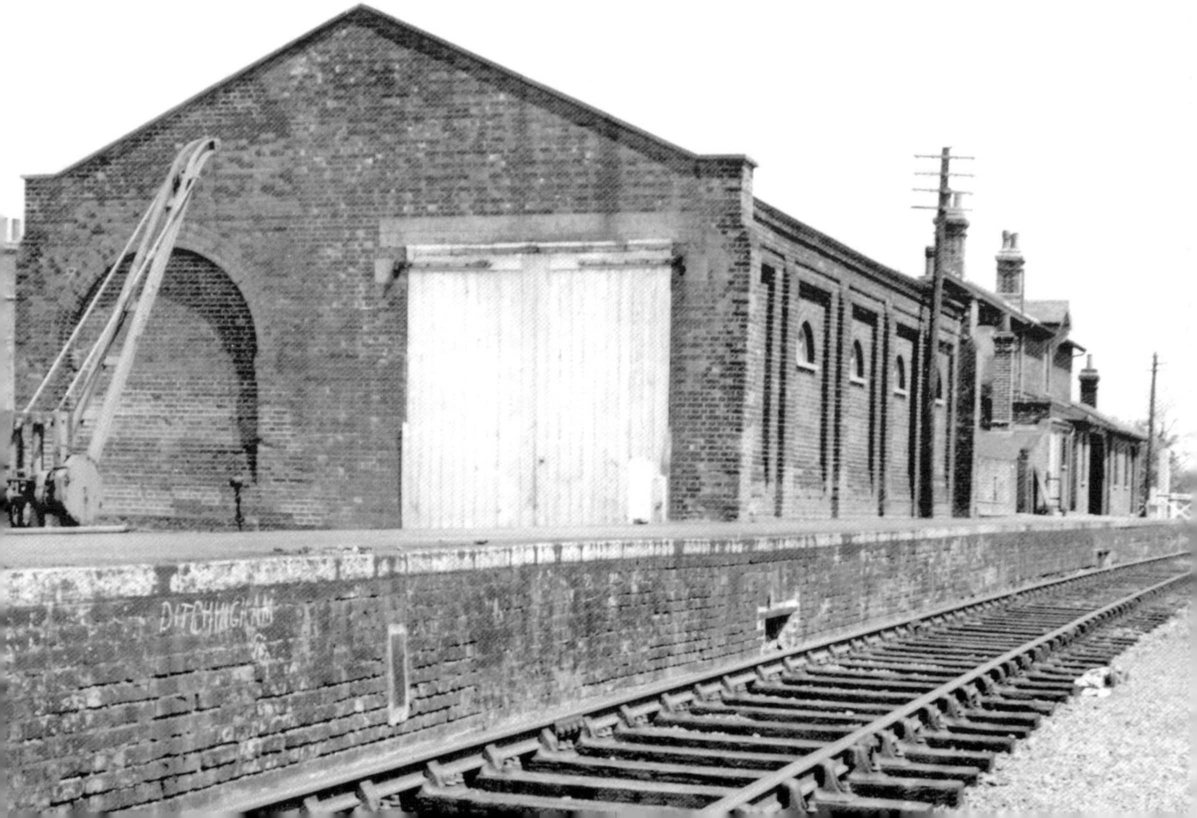
DITCHINGHAM

98. Once steam had finished, the various makes of 204 h.p. shunters were the largest type of locally allocated engines allowed. One of these is waiting to leave with five wagons piled high with sugar beet. This picture dates from the early 1960s, and we can see that the platform facing has been cut away in front of the goods shed. Goods traffic continued until 19th April 1965.
(Dr I.C.Allen/The Transport Treasury)

99. Despite the tracks having been lifted, the north side of the station building has changed little on 29th June 1969. Some twenty years earlier, a large enamel sign reading "LNER DITCHINGHAM STATION" had covered most of the wall to the left of the upstairs window. Now the walls are bare, with the exception of a bus timetable, and a poster advertising that "Bullitt", starring Steve McQueen, is showing at the Mayfair Cinema in Bungay. Eastern Counties bus route no.71 had been a direct replacement for the train service, connecting the stations at Tivetshall and Beccles with all the communities that had previously been rail-served. (P.J.Kelley)

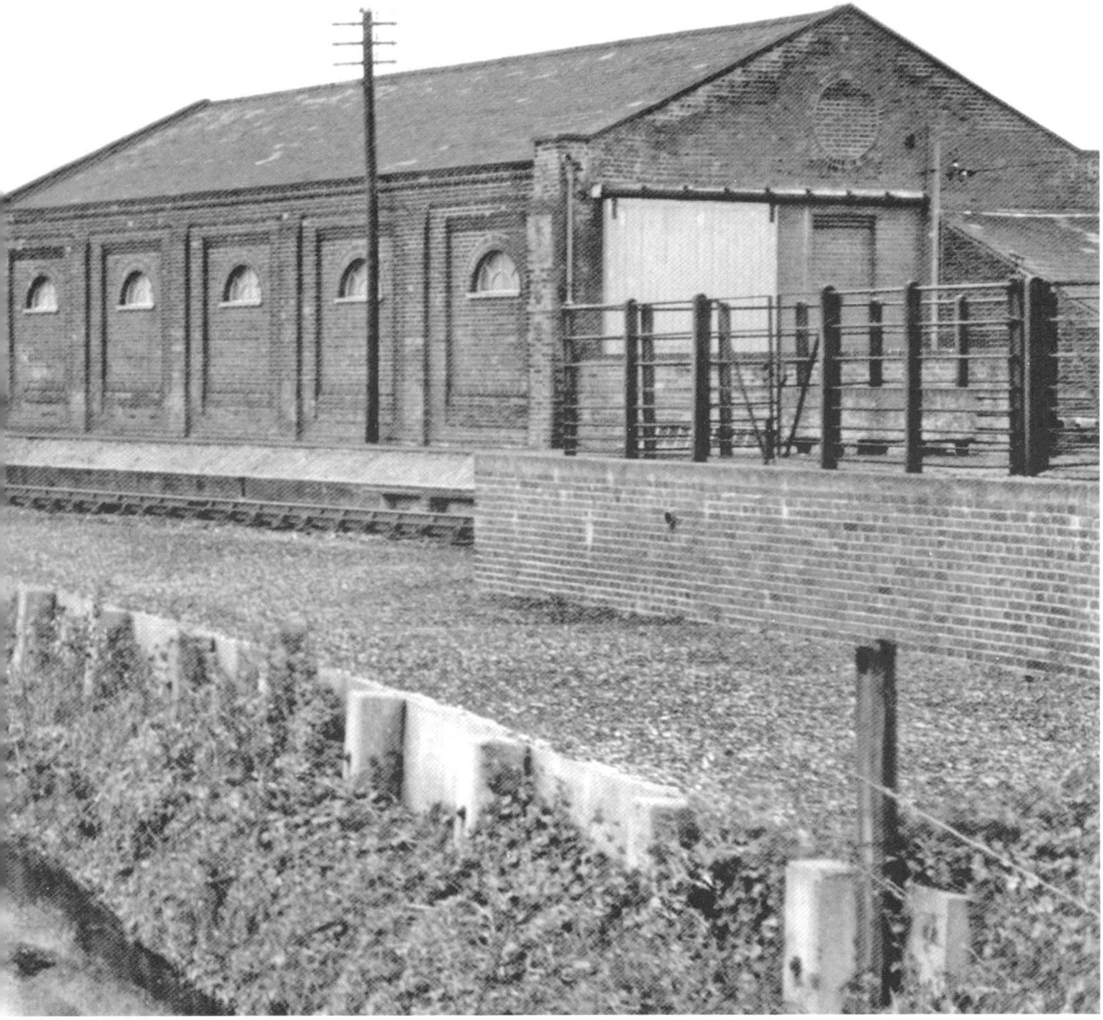

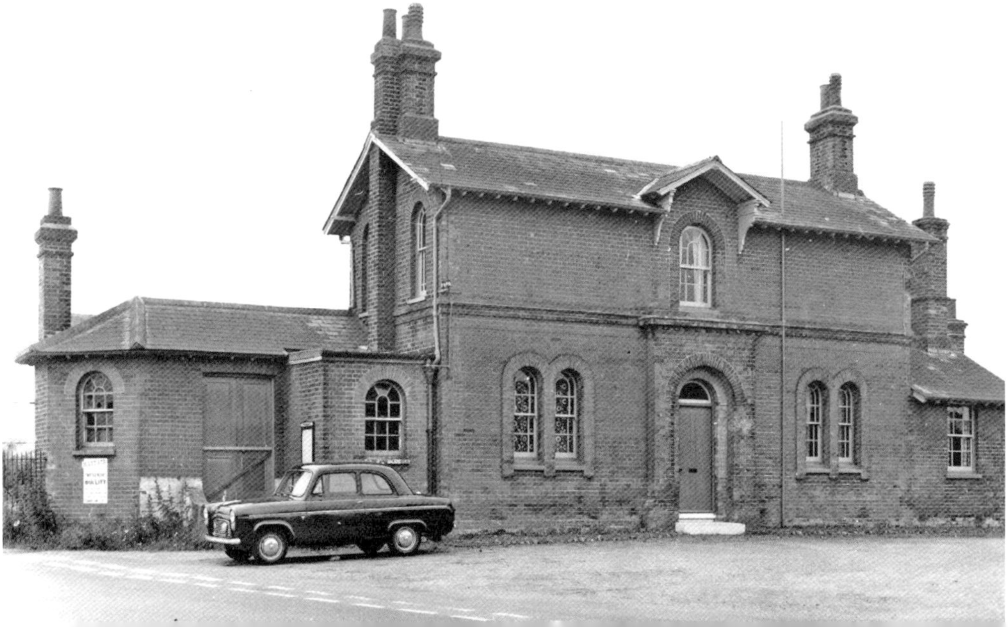

ELLINGHAM

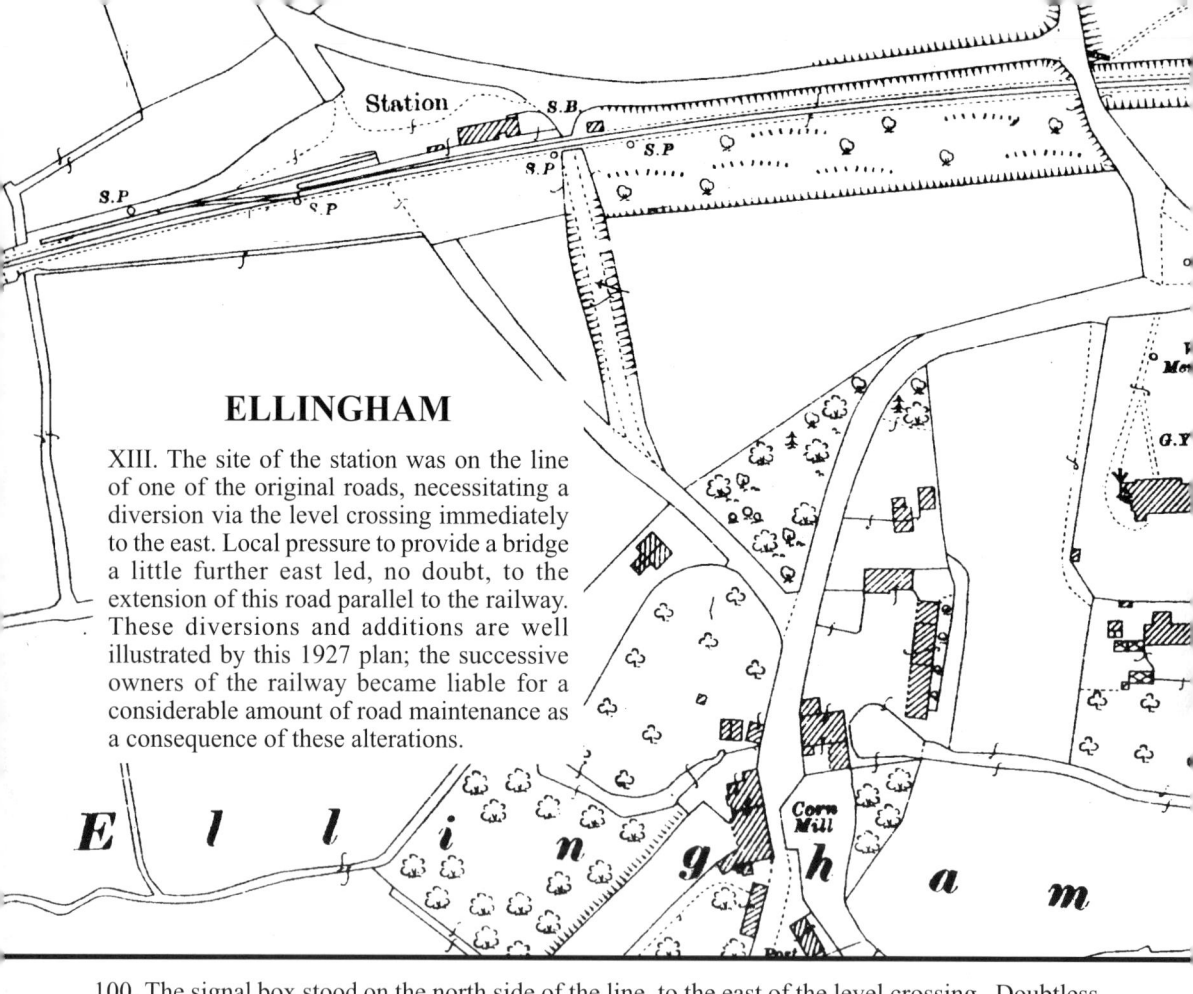

XIII. The site of the station was on the line of one of the original roads, necessitating a diversion via the level crossing immediately to the east. Local pressure to provide a bridge a little further east led, no doubt, to the extension of this road parallel to the railway. These diversions and additions are well illustrated by this 1927 plan; the successive owners of the railway became liable for a considerable amount of road maintenance as a consequence of these alterations.

100. The signal box stood on the north side of the line, to the east of the level crossing. Doubtless the signalman's busiest time was during the war years, and especially between June and September 1944, when the tiny goods yard handled some 2,518 wagons loaded with bombs for the American Air Force. This picture dates from the early 1950s, before passenger services were withdrawn. (T.Durrant)

101. On a Winter day in early 1953, the view from the level crossing shows most of what there is to see at this wayside station. The two-storey station building is supplemented by a coach body on the platform, and beyond this a few wagons are standing in the goods siding. (B.D.J.Walsh)

G. E. R.

Ellingham

102. On the same day, a former GER 2-4-2T brings the station to life as it arrives with a train from Beccles. (B.D.J.Walsh)

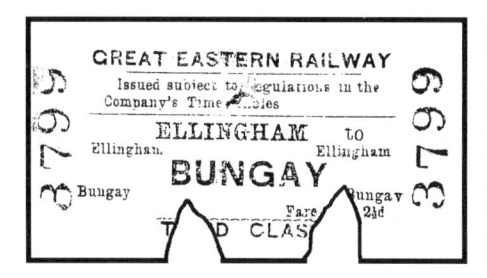

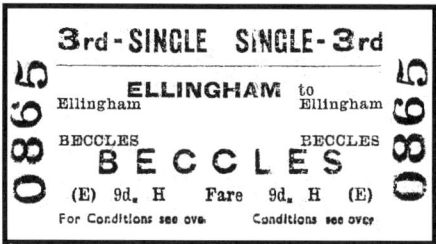

103. With the station beyond, no. D2034 heads towards Beccles with the daily goods train on 7th May 1963. The train had left Lowestoft during the morning, and was booked to shunt at the intermediate stations before arriving at Bungay at 2.07 pm. Leaving at 2.35 pm, it was allowed 30 minutes to cover the six miles back to Beccles, but as the train crew had to operate several crossing gates, this schedule was not as generous as it might appear. (Dr I.C.Allen/The Transport Treasury)

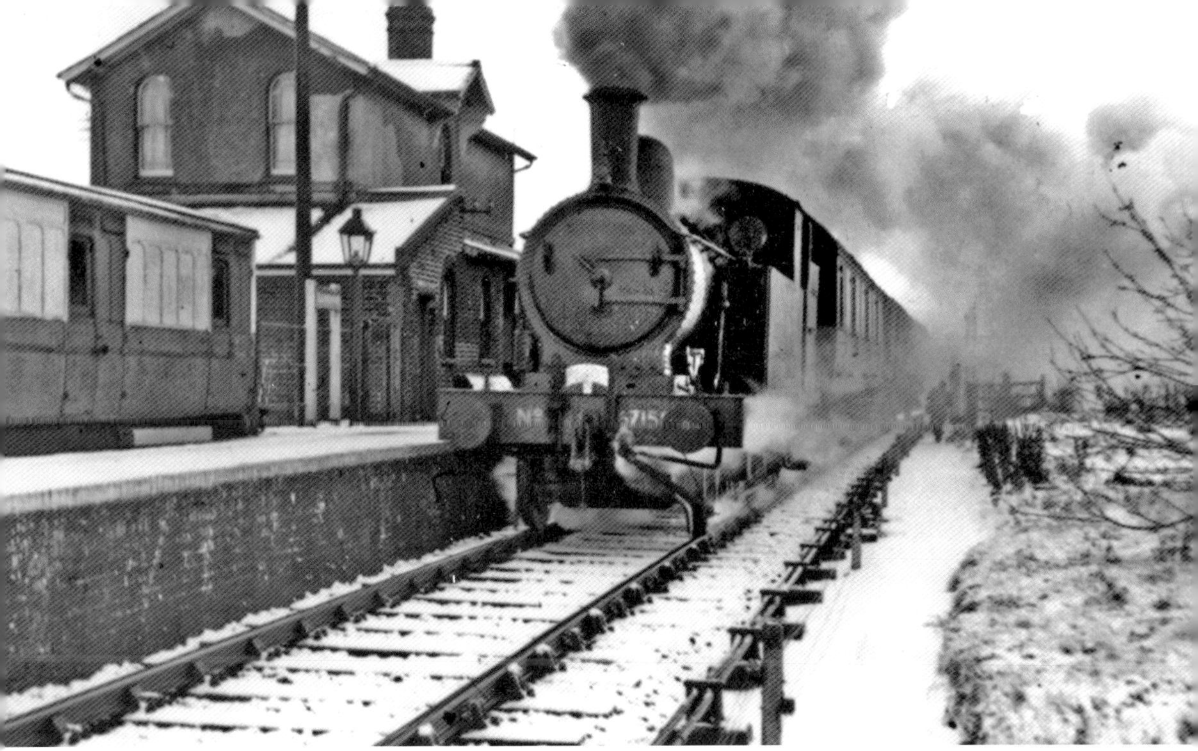

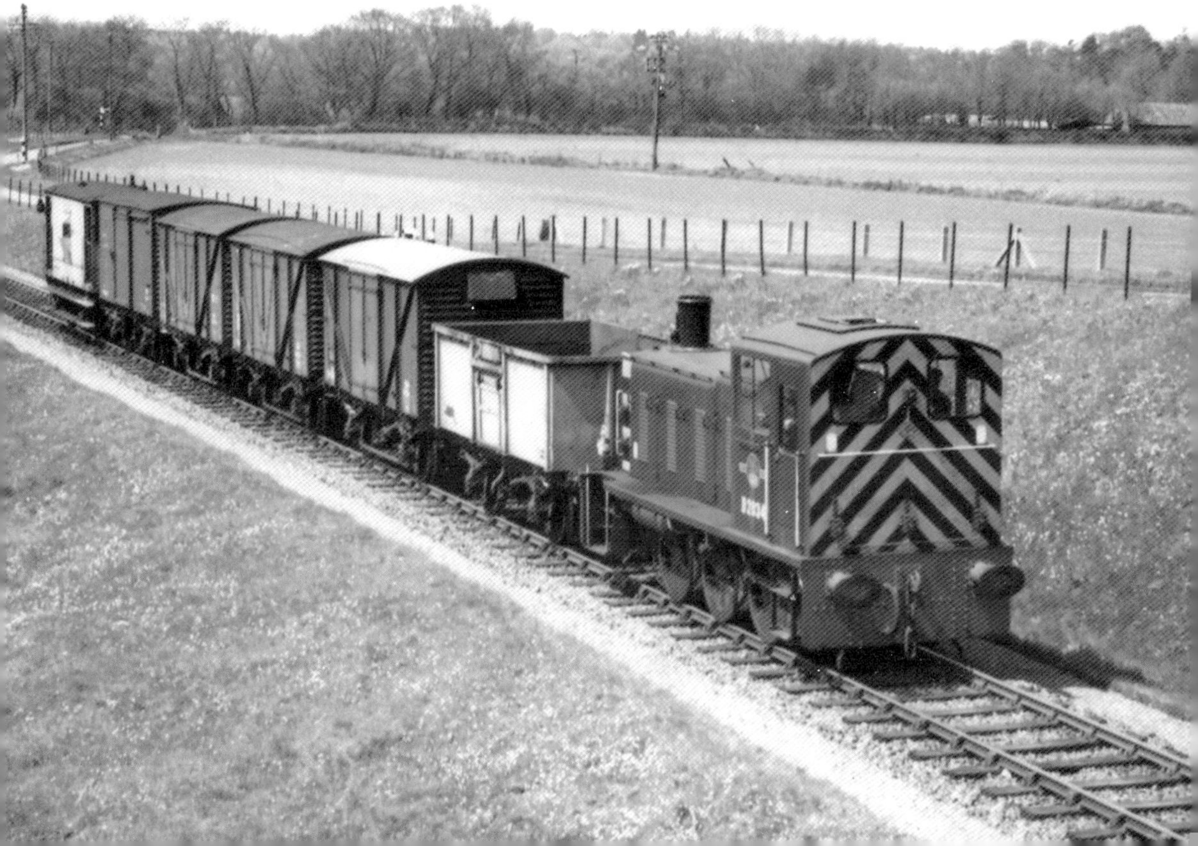

104. Illustrating the final form of trains over the line, a Hunslet shunter passes the platform with a loaded sand train around 1965. The station had lost its public goods facilities from 13th July 1964. (Dr I.C.Allen/The Transport Treasury)

⟶

105. Here, too, the line played its part in the war effort, as additional sidings were built to the east of the station in 1943/44 to serve a fuel depot, complete with storage tanks. Some 148 trains of fuel for the USAAF were received during six months in 1944 alone, and a local resident recalls that limited floodlighting enabled activity to take place around the clock. The sidings can be seen behind the gate and they remained available for use until the line was finally closed. A Hunslet shunter heads for Ditchingham with the sand empties. (Dr I.C.Allen/The Transport Treasury)

⟶

106. In later years, the station building was converted into a residence, and considerably extended. The east end of the platform and the railings provide an unaltered link with the past in November 2001. (G.L.Kenworthy)

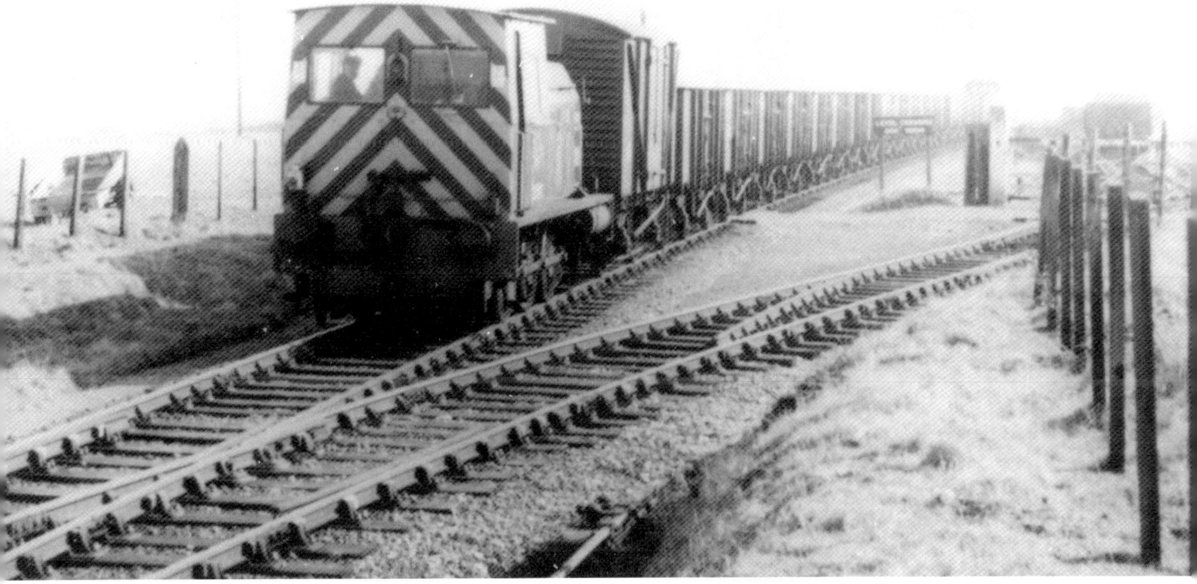

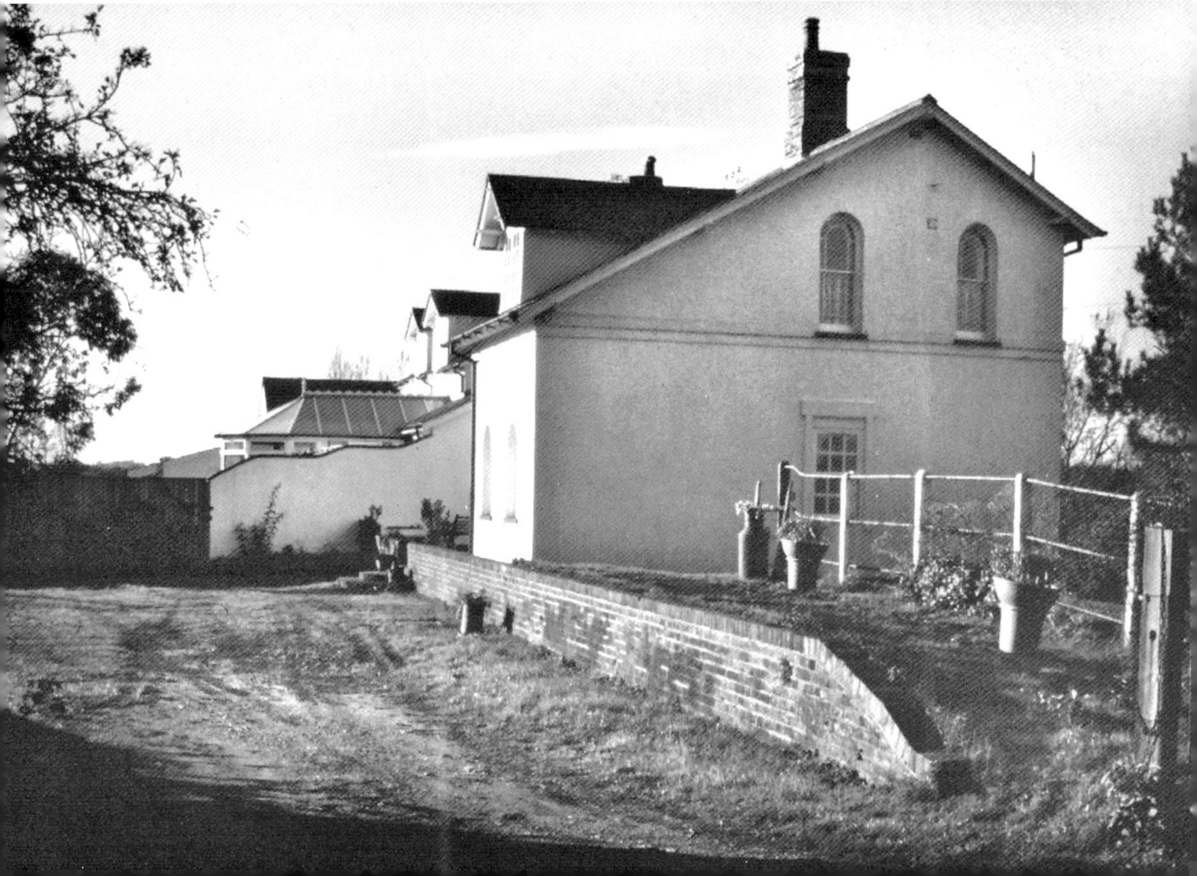

GELDESTON

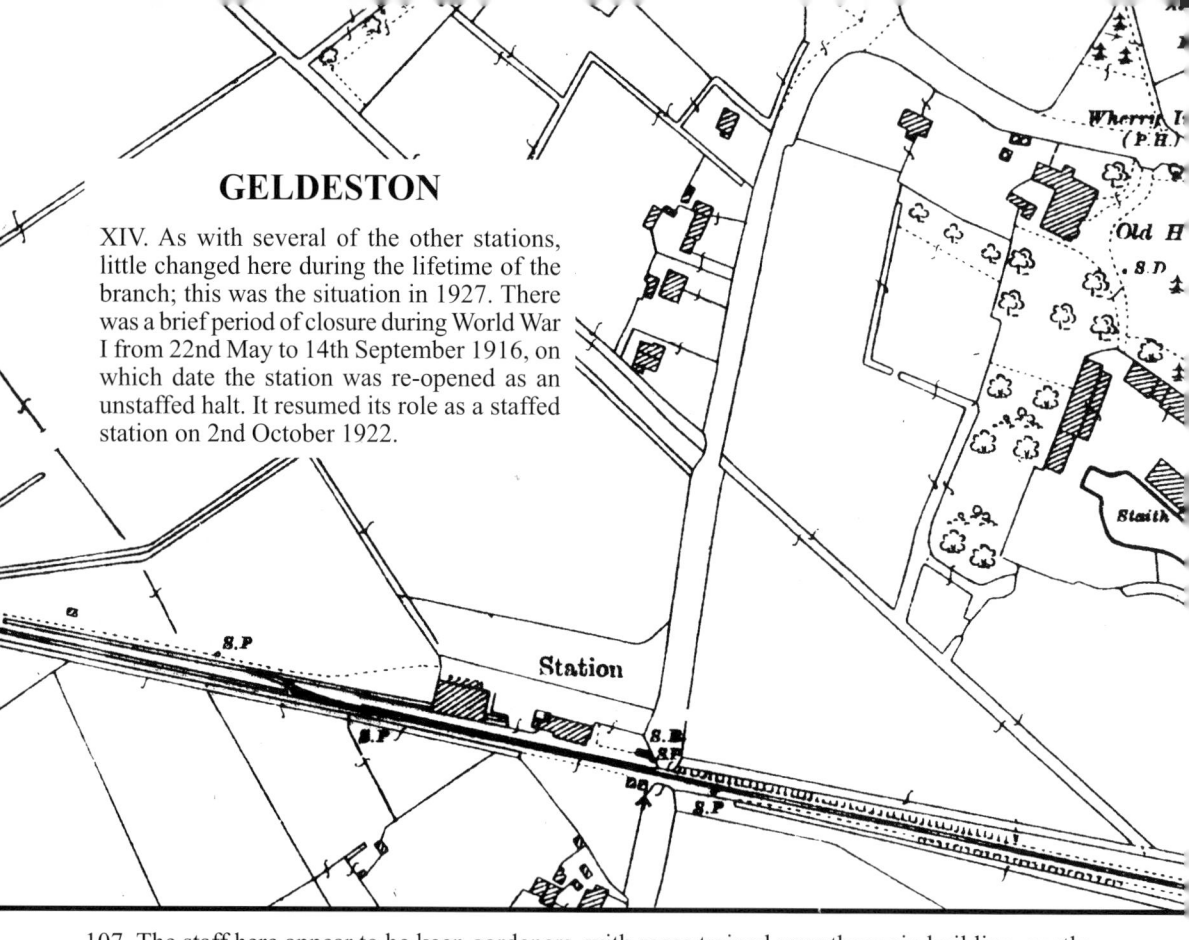

XIV. As with several of the other stations, little changed here during the lifetime of the branch; this was the situation in 1927. There was a brief period of closure during World War I from 22nd May to 14th September 1916, on which date the station was re-opened as an unstaffed halt. It resumed its role as a staffed station on 2nd October 1922.

107. The staff here appear to be keen gardeners, with roses trained over the main building, neatly tended flower beds under the running in board and boxes of plants in front of the signal box. Somebody's favourite little girl has been allowed to join the men on the platform in this peaceful scene from the early twentieth century. (P.Standley collection)

108. The few photographers who came here tended to concentrate on the main building, so this view from the west is particularly welcome. It is 12th October 1911, a typically quiet day with just one wagon standing on the single siding leading to the goods shed. Goods facilities lasted until 13th July 1964. (HMRS/H.F.Hilton collection)

109. Some forty years later, we are standing by the crossing, looking westwards. The gates are open for a train to pass, but there is no sign of any passengers. (HMRS)

110. Class F4 2-4-2T no 67158 has arrived with a train for Beccles early in 1953. Here, too, a far more modest sign has replaced the large nameboard seen in picture 107. (B.D.J.Walsh)

111. No doubt the small nameboards were provided to enable passengers from both directions to see the station name as they arrived, as there is another small sign at the west end of the station. Again, this tidy and compact scene dates from the final weeks of passenger service. (B.D.J.Walsh)

112. During the final months of operation, the loaded sand train comes to a halt next to the station building. A railwayman steps down from the Hunslet shunter before walking forward to open the level crossing gates. (Dr I.C.Allen/The Transport Treasury)

113. Both the goods shed and the station building survived into the 21st Century. Although there have been additions and modifications, the original structures are still very much recognisable in November 2001. (G.L.Kenworthy)

WEST OF BECCLES

114. From Geldeston the line ran across marshland towards the town of Beccles, standing prominently on higher ground. Just outside the town, the railway crossed the Waveney for the third and last time. Here the river is considerably broader, and pleasure craft are much in evidence as the sand train rattles across the bridge on its way back to the main line during the mid 1960s. The bridge was demolished in 1966. (Dr I.C.Allen/The Transport Treasury)

BECCLES

XV. This 1885 plan shows the situation at the junction station before considerable improvements were made in the following two decades.

115. Northgate Street was sufficiently important to justify a subway under the railway for the benefit of those pedestrians who were unwilling to wait a few minutes for the occasional train to pass over the level crossing. As we look towards the town around 1900, the entrance to the subway is between the wooden fencing and the brick wall with the letterbox. A century later, houses had been built on the trackbed, but the location could easily be traced as most of the buildings in the middle distance remained. (Beccles Museum)

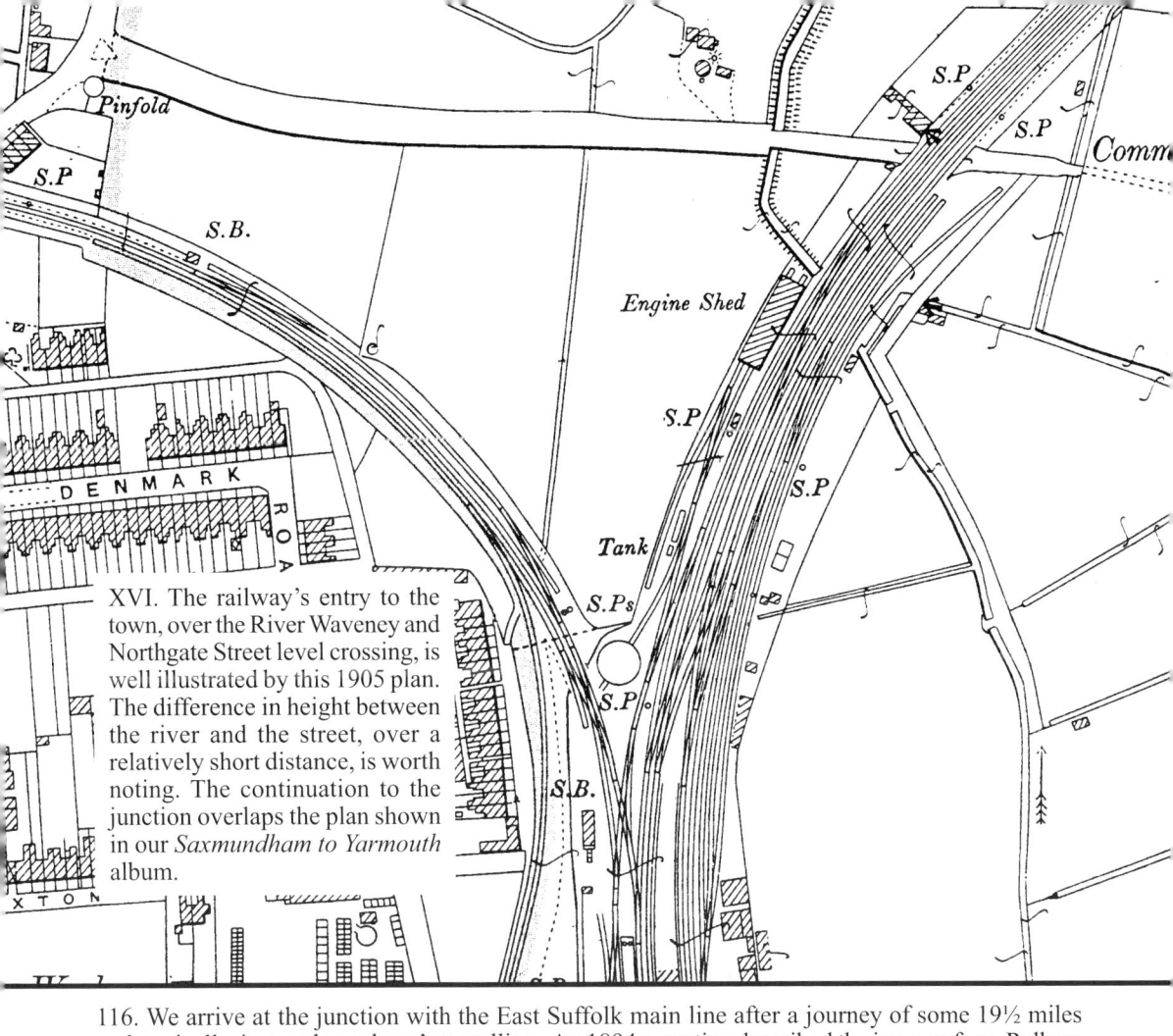

XVI. The railway's entry to the town, over the River Waveney and Northgate Street level crossing, is well illustrated by this 1905 plan. The difference in height between the river and the street, over a relatively short distance, is worth noting. The continuation to the junction overlaps the plan shown in our *Saxmundham to Yarmouth* album.

116. We arrive at the junction with the East Suffolk main line after a journey of some 19½ miles and, typically, just under an hour's travelling. An 1894 narrative described the journey from Pulham Market to Lowestoft as "at best a very tiresome one, as it entails a half-hour's wait at the pokey little station of Beccles". Matters improved following major remodelling during the 1890s, and this view, looking southwards, shows a more spacious layout in 1911.
(HMRS/H.F.Hilton collection)

117. Waveney Valley line trains normally used platform 1, the bay on the west side of the station. A very clean class J15 0-6-0, no. 65471, waits with the train for the branch, as class B1 4-6-0 no. 61205 arrives at platform 2 with a stopping train from Ipswich. (A.G.Forsyth/Initial Photographics)

118. The 9 am train for Norwich waits to leave from the bay platform on 1st September 1951. It is scheduled to take 76 minutes for the 34-mile journey, which will include 11 stops. Class E4 2-4-0 no.62789 heads a varied rake of coaches, ranging from a recent LNER steel-sided brake to a wooden-bodied clerestory roofed vehicle. (H.C.Casserley)

119. Another E4 gets its train under way and swings westwards on to the branch, passing Beccles North Junction signal box. The railway facilities here were gradually reduced over the next 30 years, and by 1984 there remained just a single line through the former down main line platform. (J.E.Dean)

120. We join the signalman in North Junction box for our final look at the Waveney Valley line. In an almost timeless scene, class J15 0-6-0 no. 65460 drifts round the curve into the station with the goods train from Bungay on an October day in 1960. (G.R.Siviour)

Middleton Press

Easebourne Lane, Midhurst, West Sussex. GU29 9AZ

A-0 906520 B-1 873793 C-1 901706 D-1 904474

OOP Out of Print - Please check current availability. **BROCHURE AVAILABLE SHOWING NEW TITLES**
Tel: 01730 813169   www.middletonpress.com   sales@middletonpress.co.uk

A
- Abergavenny to Merthyr C 91 5
- Aldgate & Stepney Tramways B 70 7
- Allhallows - Branch Line to A 62 2
- Alton - Branch Lines to A 11 8
- Andover to Southampton A 82 7
- Ascot - Branch Lines around A 64 9
- Ashburton - Branch Line to B 95 2
- Ashford - Steam to Eurostar B 67 7
- Ashford to Dover A 48 7
- Austrian Narrow Gauge D 04 7
- Avonmouth - BL around D 42 X

B
- Banbury to Birmingham D 27 6
- Barking to Southend C 80 X
- Barnet & Finchley Tramways B 93 6
- Basingstoke to Salisbury A 89 4
- Bath Green Park to Bristol C 36 2
- Bath to Evercreech Junction A 60 6
- Bath Tramways B 86 3
- Battle over Portsmouth 1940 A 29 0
- Battle over Sussex 1940 A 79 7
- Bedford to Wellingborough D 31 4
- Betwixt Petersfield & Midhurst A 94 0
- Blitz over Sussex 1941-42 B 35 9
- Bodmin - Branch Lines around B 83 9
- Bognor at War 1939-45 B 59 6
- Bombers over Sussex 1943-45 B 51 0
- Bournemouth & Poole Trys B 47 2 OOP
- Bournemouth to Evercreech Jn A 46 0
- Bournemouth to Weymouth A 57 4
- Bournemouth Trolleybuses C 10 9
- Bradford Trolleybuses D 19 5
- Brecon to Neath D 43 8
- Brecon to Newport D 16 0
- Brickmaking in Sussex B 19 7
- Brightons Tramways B 02 2
- Brighton to Eastbourne A 16 9
- Brighton to Worthing A 03 7
- Bristols Tramways B 57 X
- Bristol to Taunton D 03 9
- Bromley South to Rochester B 23 5 OOP
- Bude - Branch Line to B 29 4
- Burnham to Evercreech Jn A 68 1
- Burton & Ashby Tramways C 51 6

C
- Camberwell & West Norwood TW B 22 7
- Canterbury - Branch Lines around B 58 8
- Caterham & Tattenham Corner B 25 1
- Changing Midhurst C 15 X
- Chard and Yeovil - BLs around C 30 3
- Charing Cross to Dartford A 75 4
- Charing Cross to Orpington A 96 7
- Cheddar - Branch Line to B 90 1
- Cheltenham to Andover C 43 5
- Chesterfield Tramways D 37 3
- Chichester to Portsmouth A 14 2 OOP
- Clapham & Streatham Tramways B 97 9
- Clapham Junction - 50 yrs C 06 0
- Clapham Junction to Beckenham Jn B 36 7
- Clevedon & Portishead - BLs to D 18 7
- Collectors Trains, Trolleys & Trams B 29 2
- Crawley to Littlehampton A 34 7
- Cromer - Branch Lines around C 26 5
- Croydons Tramways B 42 1
- Croydons Trolleybuses B 73 1
- Croydon to East Grinstead B 48 0
- Crystal Palace (HL) & Catford Loop A 87 8

D
- Darlington Trolleybuses D 33 0
- Dartford to Sittingbourne B 34 0
- Derby Tramways D 17 9
- Derby Trolleybuses C 72 9
- Derwent Valley - Branch Line to the D 06 3
- Didcot to Banbury D 02 0
- Didcot to Swindon C 84 2
- Didcot to Winchester C 13 3
- Douglas to Peel C 88 5
- Douglas to Port Erin C 55 9
- Douglas to Ramsey D 39 X
- Dover's Tramways B 24 3
- Dover to Ramsgate A 78 9

E
- Ealing to Slough C 42 7
- Eastbourne to Hastings A 27 4 OOP
- East Croydon to Three Bridges A 53 3
- East Grinstead - Branch Lines to A 07 X
- East Ham & West Ham Tramways B 52 9
- East Kent Light Railway A 61 4
- East London - Branch Lines of C 44 3
- East London Line B 80 4
- East Ridings Secret Resistance D 21 7
- Edgware & Willesden Tramways C 18 4
- Effingham Junction - BLs around A 74 6
- Eltham & Woolwich Tramways B 74 X
- Ely to Kings Lynn C 53 2
- Ely to Norwich C 90 7
- Embankment & Waterloo Tramways B 41 3
- Enfield & Wood Green Trys C 03 6 OOP
- Enfield Town & Palace Gates - BL to D 32 2
- Epsom to Horsham A 30 4
- Euston to Harrow & Wealdstone C 89 3
- Exeter & Taunton Tramways B 32 4
- Exeter to Barnstaple B 15 4
- Exeter to Newton Abbot C 49 4
- Exeter to Tavistock C 82 6
- Exmouth - Branch Lines to B 00 6 OOP

F
- Fairford - Branch Line to A 52 5
- Falmouth, Helston & St. Ives - BL to C 74 5
- Fareham to Salisbury A 67 3
- Faversham to Dover B 05 7 OOP
- Felixstowe & Aldeburgh - BL to D 20 9
- Fenchurch Street to Barking C 20 6
- Festiniog - 50 yrs of change C 83 4
- Festiniog in the Fifties B 68 5
- Festiniog in the Sixties B 91 X
- Finsbury Park to Alexandra Palace C 02 8
- Frome to Bristol B 77 4
- Fulwell - Trams, Trolleys & Buses D 11 X

G
- Garraway Father & Son A 20 7 OOP
- Gloucester to Bristol D 35 7
- Gosport & Horndean Trys B 92 8 OOP
- Gosport - Branch Lines around A 36 3
- Great Yarmouth Tramways D 13 6
- Greenwich & Dartford Tramways B 14 6
- Guildford to Redhill A 63 0

H
- Hammersmith & Hounslow Trys C 33 8
- Hampshire Narrow Gauge D 36 5
- Hampshire Waterways A 84 3 OOP
- Hampstead & Highgate Tramways B 53 7
- Harrow to Watford D 14 4
- Hastings to Ashford A 37 1 OOP
- Hastings Tramways B 18 9
- Hastings Trolleybuses B 81 2
- Hawkhurst - Branch Line to A 66 5
- Hayling - Branch Line to A 12 6
- Haywards Heath to Seaford A 28 2 OOP
- Henley, Windsor & Marlow - BL to C77 X
- Hitchin to Peterborough D 07 1
- Holborn & Finsbury Tramways B 79 0
- Holborn Viaduct to Lewisham A 81 9
- Horsham - Branch Lines to A 02 9
- Huddersfield Trolleybuses C 92 3
- Hull Trolleybuses D 24 1
- Huntingdon - Branch Lines around A 93 2

I
- Ilford & Barking Tramways B 61 8
- Ilford to Shenfield C 97 4
- Ilfracombe - Branch Line to B 21 9
- Ilkeston & Glossop Tramways D 40 3
- Industrial Rlys of the South East A 09 6
- Ipswich to Saxmundham C 41 9
- Isle of Wight Lines - 50 yrs C 12 5

K
- Kent & East Sussex Waterways A 72 X
- Kent Narrow Gauge C 45 1
- Kingsbridge - Branch Line to C 98 2
- Kingston & Hounslow Loops A 83 5
- Kingston & Wimbledon Tramways B 56 1
- Kingswear - Branch Line to C 17 6

L
- Lambourn - Branch Line to C 70 2
- Launceston & Princetown - BL to C 19 2
- Lewisham & Catford Tramways B 26 X
- Lewisham to Dartford A 92 4 OOP

- Lines around Wimbledon B 75 8
- Liverpool Street to Chingford D 01 2
- Liverpool Street to Ilford C 34 6
- Liverpool Tramways - Eastern C 04 4
- Liverpool Tramways - Northern C 46 X
- Liverpool Tramways - Southern C 23 0
- London Bridge to Addiscombe B 20 0
- London Bridge to East Croydon A 58 4
- London Chatham & Dover Rly A 88 6
- London Termini - Past and Proposed D 00 4
- London to Portsmouth Waterways B 43 X
- Longmoor - Branch Lines to A 41 X
- Looe - Branch Line to C 22 2
- Lyme Regis - Branch Line to A 45 2
- Lynton - Branch Line to B 04 9

M
- Maidstone & Chatham Tramways B 40 5
- Maidstone Trolleybuses C 00 1 OOP
- March - Branch Lines around B 09 X
- Margate & Ramsgate Tramways C 52 4
- Midhurst - Branch Lines around A 49 5
- Midhurst - Branch Lines to A 01 0 OOP
- Military Defence of West Sussex A 23 1
- Military Signals, South Coast C 54 0
- Minehead - Branch Line to A 80 0
- Mitcham Junction Lines B 01 4
- Mitchell & company C 59 1 OOP
- Moreton-in-Marsh to Worcester D 26 8
- Moretonhampstead - Branch Line to C 27 3

N
- Newbury to Westbury C 66 4
- Newport - Branch Lines to A 26 6
- Newquay - Branch Lines to C 71 0
- Newton Abbot to Plymouth C 60 5
- Northern France Narrow Gauge C 75 3
- North Kent Tramways B 44 8
- North London Line B 94 4
- North Woolwich - BLs around C 65 6
- Norwich Tramways C 40 0

O
- Orpington to Tonbridge B 03 0
- Oxford to Moreton-in-Marsh D 15 2

P
- Paddington to Ealing C 37 0
- Paddington to Princes Risborough C 81 8
- Padstow - Branch Line to B 54 5
- Plymouth - BLs around B 98 7
- Plymouth to St. Austell C 63 X
- Porthmadog 1954-94 - BL around B 31 6
- Porthmadog to Blaenau B 50 2 OOP
- Portmadoc 1923-46 - BL around B 13 8
- Portsmouths Tramways B 72 3 OOP
- Portsmouth to Southampton A 31 2
- Portsmouth Trolleybuses C 73 7
- Princes Risborough - Branch Lines to D 05 5
- Princes Risborough to Banbury C 85 0

R
- Railways to Victory C 16 8
- Reading to Basingstoke B 27 8
- Reading to Didcot C 79 6
- Reading to Guildford A 47 9
- Reading Tramways B 87 1
- Reading Trolleybuses C 05 2
- Redhill to Ashford A 73 8
- Return to Blaenau 1970-82 C 64 8
- Roman Roads of Surrey C 61 3
- Roman Roads of Sussex C 48 6
- Romneyrail C 32 X
- Ryde to Ventnor A 19 3

S
- Salisbury to Westbury B 39 1
- Salisbury to Yeovil B 06 5
- Saxmundham to Yarmouth C 69 9
- Seaton & Eastbourne T/Ws B 76 6 OOP
- Seaton & Sidmouth - Branch Lines to A 95 9
- Secret Sussex Resistance B 82 0
- SECR Centenary album C 11 7
- Selsey - Branch Line to A 04 5 OOP
- Sheerness - Branch Lines around B 16 2
- Shepherds Bush to Uxbridge T/Ws C 28 1
- Shrewsbury - Branch Line to A 86 X
- Sierra Leone Narrow Gauge D 28 4
- Sittingbourne to Ramsgate A 90 8
- Slough to Newbury C 56 7

- Southamptons Tramways B 33 2 OOP
- Southampton to Bournemouth A 42 8
- Southend-on-Sea Tramways B 28 6
- Southern France Narrow Gauge C 47 8
- Southwark & Deptford Tramways B 38 3
- Southwold - Branch Line to A 15 0
- South Eastern & Chatham Railways C 08
- South London Line B 46 4
- South London Tramways 1903-33 D 10 1
- St. Albans to Bedford D 08 X
- St. Austell to Penzance C 67 2
- St. Pancras to St. Albans C 78 8
- Stamford Hill Tramways B 85 5
- Steaming through Cornwall D 30 8
- Steaming through Kent A 13 4
- Steaming through the Isle of Wight A 56 8
- Steaming through West Hants A 69 X
- Stratford-upon-Avon to Cheltenham C 25
- Strood to Paddock Wood B 12 X
- Surrey Home Guard C 57 5
- Surrey Narrow Gauge C 87 7
- Surrey Waterways A 51 7 OOP
- Sussex Home Guard C 24 9
- Sussex Narrow Gauge C 68 0
- Sussex Shipping Sail, Steam & Motor D 22
- Swanley to Ashford B 45 6
- Swindon to Bristol C 96 6
- Swindon to Newport D 30 6
- Swiss Narrow Gauge C 94 X

T
- Talyllyn - 50 years C 39 7
- Taunton to Barnstaple B 60 X 3
- Taunton to Exeter C 82 6
- Tavistock to Plymouth B 88 X
- Tenterden - Branch Line to A 21 5
- Thanet's Tramways B 11 1 OOP
- Three Bridges to Brighton A 35 5
- Tilbury Loop C 86 9
- Tiverton - Branch Lines around C 62 1
- Tivetshall to Beccles D 41 1
- Tonbridge to Hastings A 44 4
- Torrington - Branch Lines to B 37 5
- Tunbridge Wells - Branch Lines to A 32 0
- Twickenham & Kingston Trys C 35 4
- Two-Foot Gauge Survivors C 21 4 OOP

U
- Upwell - Branch Line to B 64 2

V
- Victoria & Lambeth Tramways B 49 9
- Victoria to Bromley South A 98 3
- Victoria to East Croydon A 40 1
- Vivarais C 31 1

W
- Walthamstow & Leyton Tramways B 65 0
- Waltham Cross & Edmonton Trys C 07 9
- Wandsworth & Battersea Tramways B 63
- Wantage - Branch Line to D 25 X
- Wareham to Swanage - 50 yrs D 09 8
- War on the Line A 10 X
- Waterloo to Windsor A 54 1
- Waterloo to Woking A 38 X
- Wenford Bridge to Fowey C 09 5
- Westbury to Bath B 55 3
- Westbury to Taunton C 76 1
- West Croydon to Epsom B 08 1
- West London - Branch Lines of C 50 8
- West London Line B 84 7
- West Sussex Waterways A 24 X
- West Wiltshire - Branch Lines of D 12 8
- Weymouth - Branch Lines around A 65 7
- Willesden Junction to Richmond B 71 5
- Wimbledon to Beckenham C 58 3
- Wimbledon to Epsom B 62 6
- Wimborne - Branch Lines around A 97 5
- Wisbech - Branch Lines around C 01 X
- Wisbech 1800-1901 C 93 1
- Woking to Alton A 59 2
- Woking to Portsmouth A 25 8
- Woking to Southampton A 55 X
- Woolwich & Dartford Trolleys B 66 9 OOP
- Worcester to Hereford D 38 1
- Worthing to Chichester A 06 1 OOP

Y
- Yeovil - 50 yrs change C 38 9
- Yeovil to Dorchester A 76 2
- Yeovil to Exeter A 91 6